Olivia S

THE CROCHET PROJECTS BIBLE

Publisher is provided beforehand. Any additional rights reserved.

Furthermore, the information that can be found within the pages described forthwith shall be considered both accurate and truthful when it comes to the recounting of facts. As such, any use, correct or incorrect, of the provided information will render the Publisher free of responsibility as to the actions taken outside of their direct purview. Regardless, there are zero scenarios where the original author or the Publisher can be deemed liable in any fashion for any damages or hardships that may result from any of the information discussed herein.

Contents

INTRODUCTION

Crochet is a great way to help improve your mood and creativity. You can use it to make hats, amigurumi toys, and more. But before you get started, you need some basics. Here's everything you need to know to begin crocheting! Crochet is a form of knitting. It includes rows and stitches called rounds, while knitting is a type of crochet. Rounds are the basic crochet unit, while stitches are more complex and can be used to make blankets, hats, or other items. There are five main types of crochet stitches: single crochet, double crochet, triple crochet, quadruple crochet, and even higher-level stitches that can be combined in different ways to create more intricate patterns.

Each crochet stitch has two loops on the left-hand side and one on the right-hand side. The two loops in a stitch are usually connected by a "bar" of two loops each (or sometimes just one). To make a new stitch inaccrochable (i.e., able to be crocheted through), you place the top loop of your old stitch over the bottom loop on your hook (or yarn) and work the new stitch into the old hole created by placing the old stitch over the new bar. For example, to make an Inchworm Stitch (shown below), you would put the top loop of your first stitch over the bottom loop on your hook (or yarn) and work it into the existing hole created by placing both loops over each other once (i.e., made into a bar). You can also chain multiple sets together to form an elaborate pattern like this by working them into one big hole like ch1, dc1tog(s), dc2tog(s), etc.

To complete a square Crochet square, tie off all four corners with a scrap piece of fabric or wrapping paper, then reattach using thread or yarn tail before starting crocheting around all 4 corners

Crochet is a great way to add some basic stitches to your project. To start, you will need a crochet hook and some yarn. The best way to learn how to crochet is to create a small crochet square.

Beginning crocheters will need to know how to crochet a lobster clasp. To make a lobster clasp, start by chain-casting the lobster. Then, work the loops on the first chain onto the second chain. Finally, ensure each coil is connected securely with a *link*. You'll now be able to Crochet a Lobster Clutch Foot.

To make a lobster clasp, begin by chain-casting the lobster. Then, work the loops on the first chain onto the second chain. Make sure each coil is connected securely with a *link*. You'll now be able to Crochet a Lobster Clutch Foot.

Crochet is a fun and easy way to do unique Crochet projects. By following simple crochet patterns, you can create pretty much anything you could want. Whether you're looking for a small crochet square or a big lobster clasp, plenty of options are available. Be sure to enjoy your crochet journey!

BOOK 1: Easy Beginners Projects

1.1 Crochet Double Thick Potholder

Repeatedly making a batch of these fast and straightforward crochet double-thick potholders will be something you look forward to doing. Because it utilizes just a small selection of basic crochet stitches in a simplistic arrangement, this free pattern may be constructed in a short amount of time despite its ease and simplicity. Because the cotton yarn was used in their construction, the potholders have a long lifespan and are quite practical.

Materials:

Whether you want to give them gifts, sell them at craft shows, or keep them all to yourself, you will like this crochet potholder pattern.

A ball of green yarn, a hook for crocheting in blue, and two potholders crocheted from shades of green and dark green yarn.

I like the challenge of designing crocheted products that are aesthetically pleasing and have a specific purpose. In addition, crocheting these double-thick potholders is a piece of cake, and they are the first thing that comes to mind whenever I need anything useful for the kitchen.

Procedure:

A pattern for a potholder with a diagonal opening

This pattern was passed down to me by my grandmother, who is an expert crocheter. I learned it from her.

There are a variety of names for patterns that are conceptually equivalent to crochet trivets and hot pads, such as the "magic potholder" or the "origami hot pad" pattern.

The pattern's implementation is deft, even though its premise is not very complicated. To get started with the pattern, there is a fundamental chain that you need to follow. The next thing to do is to start crocheting around the chain in a continuous circle. Because of this, the material will start to bunch up and fold in on itself.

(You could be thinking at this point that something is amiss, but you must keep on.)

When the piece of fabric has reached the desired length, it may be folded in half to produce a square potholder that is twice as thick as it was initially. You will need a crochet mat that has at least two layers to protect both your work surface and your hands from the heat that may be generated by pots and pans.

If you are interested, I have included a step-by-step guide for crocheting a beautiful potholder below.

a crochet hook in blue is being used to work on a dishcloth in a teal color.

The Model That Is Ideal for First-Time Crocheters

The following are a few of the reasons why I feel that this dishcloth would be an excellent first project for someone who crochets:

Because it requires just a few basic stitches, this free pattern is excellent for beginning crocheters. Because the pattern is straightforward to keep in mind, it is perfect for crocheting while watching television.

A single ball of cotton yarn and a few hours are all that is required to finish it. Once you have mastered the pattern, you will be able to whip up hundreds of these practical potholders in a very short amount of time.

In addition, you may gift the recipients with one of these crocheted potholders. To complement the general style of the kitchen in your house, they may be fabricated in a wide range of colors.

The Techniques Necessary to Crochet a Hot Pad

If you follow the instructions for this pattern, you will be able to crochet a square potholer that is twice as thick. The chain stitch comes first, followed by single crochet rounds, and then a mattress or whip stitch is crocheted in at the end.

The foundation chain is the first chain created while crocheting. You may work a single crochet stitch down one side of the chain and up the other side if you choose.

After you've finished laying the foundation, continue crocheting in circles using a single stitch. When I want to give my work some texture, I often stitch single crochet across the back loop of the previous row. The sides of the potholder will eventually roll over and become more elongated, creating a diagonal outline.

After that, just stitch the two sections together to create a huge, flat potholder that is twice as thick as before.

Crafting Supplies for Knitting and Crocheting Tea Cozies

The things that you need to do this work are outlined in the following paragraphs.

Silk Yarn. Choose a cotton yarn that will not fall apart even after being exposed to the high heat of the oven. In the following paragraphs, I'll share my recommendations for cotton yarns that are of the highest quality.

Hook, size H (5 mm). Using a hook size H gives me the perfect gauge for crocheting a hot pad that is not only supple and comfortable to use but also substantial enough to protect my hands from the heat. Switching to a smaller hook will let you use more yarn while still producing the dense fabric you want (G). If you have a larger hook, such as an I, you may produce a more open fabric by using less yarn.

A needle is used to thread yarn through it. You will need a tapestry needle or a yarn needle with a blunt tip to sew up the seam and weave in the ends.

As an optional add-on, you may choose fabrics that are offensive to other people. It is recommended that you insert a piece of heat-resistant Insult-Bright cloth inside the hot pad before stitching up the seam. It is not necessary to add this, however, doing so would be a nice touch if it is possible.

The Highest Grade of Cotton Yarn for Use in Making Hot Pads

When it comes to producing hot pads and potholders, cotton yarn is the material of choice. Why? When put on a hot pan, cotton yarn will not melt or burn, but acrylic yarn will not fare as well in the same situation.

The cotton yarn has several advantageous properties, including being robust, long-lasting, and easily washable. In the interest of saving, you time and effort, the dish towel may be laundered and dried with the other towels in your kitchen.

This sample was made using yarn from Lily called Sugar's Cream, which I did myself. Cotton is used in the production of this yarn, which has a worsted weight and falls under Category 4. It is offered in a kaleidoscope of colors, ranging from solids to stripes to ombres, and may be purchased.

On the other hand, you might use a different cotton yarn that has the same weight. The following is a selection of my most often-used cotton yarns for use in the kitchen:

We worked up a Dashier using crochet. This cotton yarn has a tighter twist than typical cotton yarns, which makes it less prone to splitting than regular cotton yarns. It can resist several cycles in the washing machine without losing its brand-new appearance.

Crochet and knit items for the home cook have been added.

If you like working on useful objects for the house, such as those that are displayed below, these extra crochet patterns could be something that interests you.

Washcloths for the face that are crocheted may be reused.

Trash Can Cozy that is Quick and Easy to Crochet

Two crocheted potholders, one each in teal and green, using both colors' corresponding balls of yarn.

Conceptualization of a Potholder with Two Layers of Material

Incredibly Straightforward

100 yards of cotton yarn with worsted weight (category 4) or one ball of Lily Sugar's Cream weighing between one and two ounces.

Hook size H suitable for crocheting (5 mm)

Needle for Yarn

Scissors

String & Tape Ruler

An insulated liner cloth is an option that may be put inside.

Size

A potholder that is square and is 7 inches by 7 inches. Build the basis of your potholder out of a chain that is either longer or shorter depending on how large you want the finished product to be.

Gauge

For every inch of cloth, there are 15 stitches and 10 rows.

The gauge doesn't matter all that much unless you're attempting to make a potholder of a certain size.

However, you will need to crochet at a gauge that is sufficiently tight to generate a cloth that is substantial and substantial. Using a hook size H gives me the perfect gauge for crocheting a hot pad that is not only supple and comfortable to use but also substantial enough to protect my hands from the heat. Switching to a smaller hook will let you use more yarn while still producing the dense fabric you want (G). A larger hook will not only result in a fabric that is more open and airier, but it will also use less of the yarn.

Stitches are abbreviated as "stitches."

The following is an abbreviation for each pattern stitch: Kindly be advised that the pattern is written using vocabulary common in the United States.

When crocheting, the abbreviation SC BLO refers to working entirely inside the back loops of a single stitch. Put the hook into the back loop of the stitch, then yarn over and pull through; yarn over and pull through the last two loops on the hook to complete the stitch.

Slip Stitch or SL Stitch.

Chain 40. (To make a square that is 7 inches on a side, start with a chain that is 10 inches long.)

In the first round, make a slip stitch into the second chain worked from the hook. Instead of focusing on the hump at the back, put your energy into the top loop. SC BLO in the following chain stitch until the initial chain is completely worked. To finish off the chain, add one more single crochet stitch to the very last stitch.

Continue going around in a circle and putting a single crochet stitch into each of the gaps between the chains on the side that is opposite the foundation chain. To finish, work one more single crochet stitch into the space left by the previous chain. Count: 80

using a single crochet stitch to create the starting chain of the project. Teal thread for crochet, and a blue crochet hook.

Begins successful conclusion of the first round of crochet. Needle for crocheting with yarn in blue and teal

The first round has come to an end.

At the beginning of Round 2, work a single back loop only stitch into the top of the first stitch and each stitch around. (80)

Between each stitch in rounds 3–17, a single chain stitch BLO should be crocheted (aka spiral rounds). Continue working on the piece until it is the same length as it is wide.

Continue crocheting until your project has a height of 5 inches, assuming that your original chain of 40 chain stitch stitches measured 10 inches. That works out to 17 times through for me.

A teal yarn and a blue crochet hook are being used in the process of crocheting a potholder pattern that is set against a gray background.

For the pattern of the potholder, a teal dishcloth with a blue hook is crocheted on top of a gray backdrop.

The potholder should be rolled up. To create a seam that runs diagonally, fold the top edges toward the center of the piece. Make sure that the edges will line up before you fold the paper. If you want your last stitch to be in a corner, you will need to make a couple more of those corners before you begin your last stitch.

Create a loop that may be used for suspending.

You may make a loop at the end of the potholder so that it can be hung on a hook if you want to. To do this, make a chain consisting of 12 stitches. After that, slip stitch back to the beginning of the chain at the first link.

When crocheting a pattern for a double-thick potholder, use the mattress stitch to link the diagonal edges of the piece.

Knife holder — stitch up the seams.

After cutting the yarn, you should leave a yarn tail that is about 24 inches long.

Fill in the space between the stitches on the seam. If you need to sew up a diagonal seam, you may try using a mattress stitch or a whip stitch. Both of these stitches are quite similar in appearance. The figure that follows demonstrates how a mattress stitch is done underneath one loop along each edge.

You may weave in the ends by using a yarn needle. Blocking may be done optionally.

Alterations to the Repeating Pattern

Make this layout your own by modifying it in the ways that have been suggested.

Please add more layers of insulation. The heat resistance of the potholder may be improved even further by adding an additional square of Insult-Bright that is tucked in between the layers before the seam is sewn.

An alternative to using a single strand of yarn is to use cotton yarn that has been doubled up. If you want to give this a try, you'll need a hook that's larger than normal. You might also try beginning with a chain that is a little bit shorter as the basis. To construct a potholder with a finished square measurement of 7 inches, you will need a chain that is 10 inches long.

Avoid wasting your time with SC and go instead for HDC. The whole pattern is worked in SCBLO, which, in my opinion, gives the potholder a great texture while still leaving only a few diagonal lines, even though the pattern uses all rounds. Although if you want, you may substitute any fundamental textured stitch, such as half double crochet or even single crochet, for the basic stitch known as a single crochet. Keep in mind that a higher stitch, such as half double crochet, may need fewer rounds of crochet. This is something to keep in mind while working on a project.

Change the size so that it is either larger or smaller. Depending on whether you begin by crocheting a larger or shorter chain, the finished potholder will be of a different size.

You will need a starting chain that is 8.5 inches long to produce a potholder that has a side measurement of 6 inches. When starting a chain for a square potholder measuring 8 inches, the ideal chain length is 11.5 inches.

Make a cover for a cushion out of fabric. If you were to expand it, this pattern would also be suitable for use as a cover for a cushion. If you want to build a cushion that is 18 inches in size, the chain that you start with should be 25 inches long. Before the seam has finished being stitched, the pillow form needs to be inserted.

1.2 BEGINNER'S GUIDE TO CROCHETING A SCARF

Do you have an interest in becoming an expert at crocheting scarves? If that is the case, you shouldn't think twice about using this free design since it is user-friendly and suitable for beginners. Try your hand at this straightforward pattern for a ribbed scarf to get a feel for the foundations of crochet.

Materials:

This scarf is the perfect project for you to work on, whether you are just learning how to crochet or if you are scrambling to find a gift at the last minute.

When you're done knitting your scarf, it will be toasty and cozy, exactly what you need for the cold winter days ahead. The beauty of this simple pattern is that it can be personalized in any way you want by altering the color of the yarn, adding fringe, or making it more prominent. Next step: you decide. Let's get our crochet hooks out and get started!

Procedure:

a chunky crocheted scarf in a light cream tone

Making simple rectangular objects, like this crochet scarf pattern, allowed me to gain experience in the trade. Because of how straightforward this pattern is to execute; I often recommend it to beginners who have just mastered the fundamentals of crochet and are looking for their first "serious" item to work on with the needle.

When disassembled into their component pieces, scarves are nothing more than highly long rectangles, which are substantial gauge swatches. While crocheting a scarf isn't more challenging than crocheting a gauge swatch, wearing a scarf is a far more satisfying experience.

Free Instruction on How to Crochet a Scarf

With the aid of this free crochet pattern, you can whip up a ribbed scarf that gives the impression of being challenging but is, in reality, relatively simple. It is an excellent approach for teaching beginners the principles of crochet without causing them to get disheartened in the process.

It won't matter if you've never picked up a hook in your life since our instructions are so precise that you won't miss a thing even if you do. You just need a fundamental knowledge of crochet stitches and some experience reading crochet patterns to get started.

This trendy unisex scarf is a perfect first crochet project for beginners since it only requires the chain stitch and the half double crochet stitch to complete (half double crochet). We will walk you through the procedure, beginning with the chain stitch and ending with the fringe.

If you want to improve your crochet skills or if you're looking for a quick project, this easy-to-follow scarf pattern is perfect for you. That is not even the most critical aspect! The process takes around two hours, beginning with the first step and ending with the last.

After getting the hang of this straightforward ribbed scarf pattern, you may want to try cropping a hat or one of the many other crochet accessories, such as a headband or a cowl.

The scarf's color is cream, with a substantial yarn and a gray background.

The Design's Official Documentation

Because it is crocheted with a large hook and a substantial yarn, the scarf may be completed relatively quickly. People believe it can be produced in two to three hours, making it ideal for a weekend project or a gift to give at the last minute.

For this project, you will need two whole Wool-Ease Thick and Quick yarn skeins. (If the "yarn chicken" game makes you nervous, don't hesitate to get that additional ball.)

Because of its thick yarn and ribbed shape, this scarf offers a high level of comfort and keeps the wearer warm. The wintertime is the perfect time to take advantage of this attractive option.

Different scarf patterns that may be downloaded for free here: In addition, for people who are as enthusiastic about crochet scarves as I am, I have assembled a compilation of 25 of the free crochet scarf patterns that I consider to be among the best.

One kind of Pattern Stitch is known as HDC Ribbing.

The ribbing that runs throughout the length of the scarf's main body is worked using the "half double crochet in the back loops alone" (abbreviated HDC BLO).

The location of the hook insertion is the only thing that differentiates this ribbing design from the regular half-double crochet stitch. Instead of inserting the hook under both the front and back loops of each stitch, only insert it beneath the back loop alone.

An elastic fabric perfect for scarves may be produced by working solely into the back loops of a half-double crochet ribbing. This creates ribbing. It knits up into a soft cloth that gives the impression of being knit.

Pictures showing where the crochet hook should be placed to work just in the back loop of a crocheted row

It is not a problem if you have never worked with HDC BLO before. I will explain how to make this crocheting method and show you how to do it in the following pattern.

Different Scarf Designs

The following are some tips for customizing the layout to suit your preferences.

You only need to change the directions for the design if you want the scarf to be a different length.

To make a shorter scarf, the initial chain should be narrower, with fewer stitches overall. Work the first chain of stitches for a longer scarf using more stitches.

The ends of the scarves that have been shortened would look great with fringe. The amount of frame you wish to add will determine whether or not you need a third skein of yarn for the project.

Infinity scarves of crochet may be created by attaching the two shorter ends of the scarf. If you stitch the two ends of the scarf together, you will create a large loop of fabric suitable for going around your neck not once but twice.

This bundle includes all the equipment and materials you will need to perform the current activity successfully.

A highly dense and substantial kind of yarn

Crochet hook, size N (9mm)

Hooks and Needles for Crocheting (like a blunt-tipped tapestry needle)

Scissors

String & Tape Ruler

You're interested in crocheting this scarf, but you're not sure how much yarn you'll need. To complete this project, you will need about two skeins of Wool-Ease Thick Quick. Get a couple of extra skeins of yarn if you want your completed scarf to be longer or if you want to add fringe to it. You can do any of these things by getting additional yarn.

The Most Luxurious Yarn Available for Making Extra-Large Scarves.

This pattern was designed using one of my all-time favorite yarns, Lion Brand Wool-Ease Thick and Quick, and it was produced with that yarn. This lovely yarn in a bulky weight works up fast, making it an excellent choice for projects that need to be knitted or crocheted at the last minute.

Because it provides the warmth of wool while requiring just a fraction of the care that acrylic does, this yarn is ideal for making winter accessories. Because it is made of acrylic and wool, it is fluffy, affordable, and straightforward to care for. It is also important to note that this particular yarn is offered in more than fifty colors.

You are allowed to use any other yarn you choose in its stead if you like. Make sure you prepare by making a gauge swatch, and keep in mind that the size of the hook you use may need to change based on the kind of yarn you choose.

The following list contains alternative yarns that may be used for this project.

If you're going to be roving, make sure you get the Wool-Ease Roving from Lion Brand Yarn.

Heavy and brisk in the Midwestern United States

The location of the renowned Lion Brand Factory in the United States

Stitch that's Super Bulky and Mighty

If you don't have any super bulky yarn on hand, you might try using two strands of thicker worsted-weight yarn that are tied together instead of a single super bulky yarn.

This a straightforward pattern for a crocheted scarf, made in half-double crochet with some cream yarn and an orange crochet hook.

The Very Best Hooks to Use When Crocheting

You're going to need a crochet hook as well. My go-to crochet hooks are the ergonomic versions made by Clover. Because of how easy it is to use; they are perfect for those who have never done anything like this before.

Another of my most cherished possessions is this exquisite set of crochet hooks designed by Furls and crafted of wood. They are pliable and comfortable, making them a delight to put on and take off.

For this particular endeavor, you will need an N/M 9mm hook. You may need an N/P 10.0mm hook to handle the tight crocheting you're doing.

How Long Should a Crochet Scarf Be, Roughly Speaking?

You have complete control over the size of the finished crochet scarf you create. You may adjust the length of your scarf by determining how many times you want to wrap it around your neck. This can be done in one of two ways.

Scarves that are crocheted often range from sixty to seventy inches in width. It is customary for a crocheted scarf to be the same length as the person wearing it. It is possible to wrap the scarf around the wearer's neck at least once.

This design was supposed to be 66 inches long, about five feet and fifty inches.

Instructions for Making a Chunky Scarf Using Crochet

The Process of Defining the Template

When it comes to the level of complexity, this exercise is perfect for beginners.

The finishing measurements for a scarf that is appropriate for an adult are 66 inches in length and 6 inches wide.

Work 7.5 stitches in HDC BLO over a square of 4 inches. This will give you the correct gauge.

A little less than two skeins of yarn. You may work with Lion Brand Wool-Ease Thick and Quick (Category 6) or any comparable, exceptionally bulky yarn.

Hook, 9 mm N/M or size required to achieve gauge for a job.

Additional materials consist of the following:

Needles suitable for working with yarn or tapestry

scissors

stitch indicators that are unnecessary to use

If you like, you may use a gauge; otherwise, a tape measure will serve.

Various Symbols, as well as Stitches

"Stitches," "stitch," and "stitches" are all homonyms.

Chain stitching is also known as chain stitching.

a pair of stitches worked in half double crochet

Only loops in the opposite direction (BLO)

Detailed Embroidery Work

An almost unbroken string of stitches will be worked through the reverse side of the cloth. In the design, you may shorten this to BLO if you want.

It displays the V-shaped loops created at the top of each crochet stitch by holding up a swatch of fabric in front of the audience.

What precisely do you mean when you state "back loop only" in your sentence?

A row of crochet stitches looks like a sequence of small Vs. When seen from above. Crochet stitches are worked in rows. The V segment closest to you when you hold a piece of crochet fabric with the V's facing up is known as the front loop, while the portion of the V that is farthest from you is known as the back loop.

When beginning a new stitch, place your hook under both the front and back loops of the previous stitch. When working most of the stitches in this pattern, you will enter the theme behind the stitch rather than through the initial loop at the front of the work.

Observe and Make Notations on a Pattern

The design utilizes the language of the United States of America as its primary language choice.

The scarf is knit in a flat pattern, using longitudinal rows knitted both forwards and backward.

The turning chain for stitch two is skipped over when calculating the number of stitches.

Even though most of the half-double crochet stitches will be worked through the back loop, you may obtain a neater edge by performing each row's first and final half-double crochet stitches beneath both loops. This is true even though most half-double crochet stitches will be worked in the back loop.

The Process of Making a Scarf

I am starting with a simple slip knot. A slip knot is the attachment point between the crochet hook and the yarn.

The slip knot is created by wrapping the yarn in a light cream hue around a crochet hook in bright orange color.

A Slip Knot Tie-Down Guide

To begin, take your yarn and make a loop, being sure to leave a 6-inch tail at the end.

Insert the crochet hook in a front-to-back motion into the middle of the loop.

Get a grip on the tail of the yarn, also known as the ball end, and wind it into a circle.

Pull on the yarn from both ends to make the slip knot more secure.

Create a chain of stitches to start with. Crochet.

The next step in crocheting is to create the foundation chain for the scarf you are crocheting. A starting chain sometimes referred to as a foundation chain, is a series of crochet chain stitches that acts as the foundation for the rest of the scarf. A beginning chain may also be called a foundation chain.

Creating a chain stitch entails the following steps:

You can create a loop by putting the hook into the slip knot, passing the yarn over the theme, and then drawing a circle through the space created by the turn.

Repeat the instructions from the previous section to create as many chains as you want.

Are you chaining too closely? You may try making the foundation stitches using a hook that is 10mm or 12mm in size and then transitioning to a theme that is 9mm for the rest of the scarf.

This pattern calls for a total of 126 chains to be completed successfully.

A valuable piece of advice for novice crocheters is to exclude the slip knot and the hook formed while calculating their chains.

Row 1

Crocheting stitches are worked into the foundation chain to make the first row. Inserting the crochet hook from the front to the back into the first stitch of the starting chain is how you start crocheting. Just insert the tip of the pin into the hollow of the V.

You may also turn the chain over and work the first row of stitches into the raised regions on the back. This would be an alternative option. It is up to you to determine whether or not you think a project will have a more polished appearance if it is completed by working into the back bar of the item being created.

Photos that demonstrate the two spots where the crochet hook is put to work into the foundation chain stitches.

These two places are depicted under the top loop and the rear hump.

Work 124 half double crochets across, beginning in the chain three chains away from the hook. Turn. (124sts) (124sts)

Remembering the turning chain does not need to be counted as a stitch while working with this pattern is essential.

A crochet hook and some yarn in a brilliant orange color provide a striking contrast against the background of gray.

Starting with foundation half-double crochet stitches is an alternative to the typical long beginning chain. More expert crocheters may prefer this method since it requires less concentration. Build a foundation consisting of 124 whole half double crochet stitches if you want to work from the bottom up rather than the top down.

Row 2

In the second row, you will only work half-double crochet in the front and back loops of the stitch. However, you will use a traditional half double crochet in the start and last stitches of the row.

Chain 2 to start the second row (does not count as a stitch). Please start with the first stitch and work one-half double crochet into it. Create 122 single and double crochets alone in the back loop. Complete the project by performing a half-double crochet stitch on the last stitch. Turn (124 stiches) (124 stiches)

After just two rows of half-double crochet working exclusively in the back loops, a simple crochet scarf was finished.

Rows 3-10

Row 2 will be repeated for the required number of rows to get the width you want for your scarf.

Rows 3-10 are worked with two chains (does not count as a stitch). Please start with the first stitch and work one-half double crochet into it. Create 122 single and double crochets alone in the back loop. Complete the project by performing a half-double crochet stitch on the last stitch. Turn (124 stiches) (124 stiches)

It is essential to consider that the width of your scarf may be modified by altering the number of crocheted rows.

Finishing

When you have finished the last row of the project, you should snip the yarn and then secure it in a knot. Thread the adventure ends through a crochet needle or a tapestry needle with a blunt tip to weave them in.

This is it! You've just completed knitting a simple scarf, so you should be proud of yourself.

A finished cream-colored crocheted scarf on a background of a subdued gray tint.

The following are several different ways to tie a scarf such that it seems to have been done by a professional.

Option 1: Complete the Look by Fringing the Edges

The shorter ends of the scarf may have fringe added to them, although doing so is entirely optional.

For fringe, you will need forty separate strands of yarn, each measuring 12 inches in length. Create a loop in the string by folding it in half lengthwise. Check that the ends are correctly aligned with one another.

When beginning a crochet stitch, the hook should be inserted from the back into the front of the work. You may use the theme to get a hold of two strands of yarn just where they fold over on themselves.

Pulling on the yarn ends is the only way to get them to pass halfway through the stitch you're working on.

Run the ends of the yarn through the loops that have been crimped.

Pulling on the yarn ends will make the fringe more compact.

As a secondary option, we offer the Infinity Scarf Variation.

When working with crochet, all required to create an infinity scarf is to produce a loop by attaching the two short ends. First, bring the two short ends of the scarf together so that they are aligned, and then use a mattress stitch to attach them.

1.3 CHUNKY RIBBED BEANIE CROCHET HAT PATTERN

This straightforward pattern for a Ribbed Beanie is all you need to start crocheting hats. This crochet beanie with the appearance of knit ribbing was created using a simple stitch pattern that is simple and easy to recall. The completed piece is nicely crocheted yet has the softness and suppleness of knitting. Because it only takes one skein of bulky-weight yarn, it is ideal for crocheters of any skill level.

Materials:

This crochet hat pattern is great for someone just starting out or for anybody seeking a project that they can work on quickly and efficiently while watching their favorite program on Netflix.

A crocheted beanie in a bright yellow color finished with a ribbed knit structure and a pom in white.

The Ribbed Beanie is a simple crochet project that provides a lot of enjoyment but can be completed in a short amount of time. I designed this unisex beanie pattern using the most basic knitting stitches and techniques, so it is perfect for those just starting the craft. In my opinion, this is the most straightforward crochet hat pattern that novices can use.

Because of the substantial yarn and the beautiful texture, this beanie is perfect for wearing throughout the cold winter months. Because you only need a little portion of a skein of thick yarn to make it, the cost to do so is relatively low.

The stitch pattern for this easy beanie is relatively uncomplicated, so it won't take you long to finish it.

I'll show you how to adjust the design so that it may be worn by a broad range of people, from tiny children to very tall adults.

Don't overlook that every family member will welcome a new beanie! I crochet a cap for every person on my list of people to give gifts to for Christmas, and I like making this specific kind of hat.

Procedure:

After this, you may crochet a short scarf with your brand-new headpiece. This is by far the most excellent pattern for a crochet scarf I've ever seen, and it's easy enough for a beginner yet sophisticated enough for an experienced crocheter.

The Design's Official Documentation

You will fall head over heels for this crochet hat since it is so easy and quick to make. This location lacks any elaborate needlework. The only stitches used in this pattern are the chain stitch, the single crochet stitch, and the half double crochet stitch.

This fashionable crochet beanie will keep your head toasty thanks to the plush yarn used in its construction. In addition, it is knitted in a flexible ribbing stitch pattern, resulting in a snug but comfortable fit for the wearer.

This modern crocheted hat may be fashioned in a square or rectangular shape. After the opening has been gathered and the long sides have been sewn together, the cap is finished and ready to wear.

Therefore, you should be able to produce this beanie if you know how to crochet in rows.

The Crochet Version of the Rib Stitch

The ribbing pattern for the main body of the hat is made in half-double crochet, and the cap is crocheted in one continuous piece.

By working the half-double crochet stitch through the back loop of the stitch alone, you may make a flexible crochet ribbing for hats.

I put a few single crochet stitches onto the top of the hat so that it would have a more natural taper. This helped the hat fit better. This will be helpful when it comes time to secure the hat's crown.

Alterations to the Repeating Pattern

The overall shape may be readily adjusted to accommodate a wide variety of head circumferences, from an adult to a child. I have a hat size guide and a straightforward method that ensures a secure but comfortable fit every time.

I designed the hat 12 inches tall so that it would be able to handle a broad brim that I layered on top of each other. I will show you how to modify the pattern, so the hat's brim doesn't get creased up while you wear it.

This beanie follows a more conventional design and does not have an overly drooping appearance.

This hat is characterized by its knitted-like appearance, flexible ribbing, and thick crochet construction.

Most Suitable Fibre for Large Knit Hats

Because Lion Brand Color Made Easy is one of my all-time favorite yarns, you'll see that I used it while designing this pattern. The speed with which this thick yarn can be knitted makes it an excellent choice for rapid projects.

This yarn comprises many strands, resulting in a thick texture with well-defined stitches.

Because it is made entirely of acrylic, it is not only fluffy but also affordable and needs a reduced amount of upkeep. This yarn is available in more than twenty beautiful colors to choose from.

Please take notice that we can no longer provide you with this yarn. You are welcome to substitute it with any other string you choose so long as it has a thick weight. Make sure you prepare by making a gauge swatch, and keep in mind that the size of the hook you use may need to change based on the kind of yarn you choose.

The following list contains alternative yarns that may be used for this project.

Knit beanie with an elastic ribbed pattern, including a fold-over brim and cuff.

Crochet Cap Measurement Guide

Do you want to know how large of a hat you should make? If you wish for your crochet hat to look good and feel comfortable on your head, you should make it a little bit smaller than the diameter of your head. As the cap grows to its full size, this will ensure that it fits securely while being comfortable.

You may choose the size that will suit you best by using a measuring tape to take measurements across the broadest part of your head. The number that you get is the circumference of your head.

The final hat size may then be calculated by taking this amount and subtracting about three inches from it. Because of the elasticity of the stitch pattern, I've found that three-inch negative ease yields a comfortable, form-fitting garment that can be worn without compromising on style.

Take, for example

For illustration's sake, the circumference of my skull is 23 inches, which positions me smack dab amid the Adult Medium and Adult Large categories. After considering the negative ease of three inches, the hat should have a diameter of twenty inches when it is done.

I wanted a finished hat size of 20 inches for my beanie, so I crocheted 36 rows plus one seaming row to get there. This gave me a completed hat size of 20 inches.

What does it mean to have "ease" while crocheting?

In crochet patterns, the size difference between the completed object and the person crocheting it is denoted by the word "ease," which stands for "ease." Negative ease indicates that the finished garment will be smaller than the wearer but will stretch to accommodate the wearer.

Depending on the stitch pattern and the yarn's elasticity, crocheted hats often have negative ease of between two and seven centimeters (three and three-and-a-half inches).

A Guide to the Sizes of Beanies and Other Ribbed Headwear

The Craft Yarn Council has provided the following table with information on the standard circumferences of various-sized heads. I have also added a column for the final hat size, considering the exact 3 inches of negative ease as before.

To get the correct length measurement for the hat, you must crochet the needed number of chains. Add extra 2.5 inches to this overall measurement, so you have room for the folded brim.

After that, continue crocheting around the hat's circumference until it is the size you want it to be.

A crocheted beanie in the brilliant color yellow worked in a ribbing stitch pattern that is modern and streamlined.

Pattern for a Beanie Made with Ribbed Stitching to Crochet

When it comes to the level of complexity, this exercise is perfect for beginners.

The final design includes instructions for all ages and sizes, from infant to adult.

My starting point for this design will be an Adult Medium, which translates to a hat that is 12 inches long and has a diameter of 20 inches.

For a square of 4 inches on each side, use needles of size 12 and a crochet or knitting pattern with 7.5 rows. Taking your gauge measurement might be of assistance to you if you are uncertain about your size.

Ideal for this project is a yarn with a bulky weight, such as Color Made Easy by Lion Brand (Category 5). I estimated that the target was somewhere between 100 and 200 yards away.

Hook Size K-10.5 (6.5mm) for Knitters or Crocheters, or the Size Hook Necessary to Achieve the Desired Gauge

Additional materials consist of the following:

Needle for yarn

stitch indicators that are unnecessary to use

If you like, you may use a gauge; otherwise, a tape measure will serve.

Various Symbols, as well as Stitches

"Stitches," "stitch," and "stitches" are all homonyms.

Chain stitching is also known as chain stitching

must be worked in the round

a pair of stitches worked in half double crochet

Only loops in the opposite direction (BLO)

Detailed Embroidery Work

The construction of this hat does not need any particularly unique stitches. However, you should know that working exclusively in back loops is the abbreviation BLO. In the design, you may shorten this to BLO if you want.

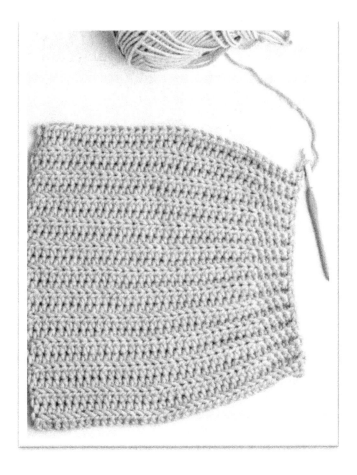

Observe and Make Notations on a Pattern

The design utilizes the language of the United States of America as its primary language choice.

You will work the hat in rows in both directions while it is flat.

After the flat component has been finished, it will be seamed into a tube.

After that, the characteristic shape of the hat is accomplished by collecting one of the ends.

The Process of Creating a Pattern

In the following paragraphs, you will find comprehensive directions for constructing a cozy hat out of crochet yarn to wear throughout the cooler months.

Getting my measurements was the first thing that needed to be done. I'm looking for a fedora-style hat with a brim that's 12 inches long and has a head circumference of 20 inches when it's finished.

Chain 36 stitches to begin the first row. Begin the next set of 30 half double crochet stitches on the chain two chains away from the hook. A total of five rows were worked in single crochet—35 stitches after the turn.

Row 2: Chain one, turn, and work five single crochets into the back loop only of the first stitch. Following, work thirty double crochets into the back loop only of the next 29 stitches. Turn. (Stitches: 35)

The third row is worked as follows: chain 1, then working in the same stitch as the chain, work 30 half double crochet stitches in the back loop alone, followed by four single crochet stitches in the back loop alone, and finally one single crochet stitch. Turn. It took a total of 35 stitches to complete.

The enchantment of the half-double crochet stitch worked via the back loop to create a flexible crochet beanie.

You should continue to repeat rows 2 and 3 until the long edge of your crochet piece reaches 19.5 inches or until it is roughly 1/2 inch shorter than the length you specified for the finished hat. Once you have reached this measurement, you should stop working on the item.

The crocheting on my hat extends for a total of 36 rows. The last row of seaming will add the remaining half an inch in length to ensure that everything fits perfectly.

It is important to note that the long edge of the half-double crochet stitches, not the long edge of the single crochet threads, should be utilized for this measurement. A flexible fabric measuring tape would suit this situation better than a brutal ruler.

Stitch the side seams together as the very final step.

What a burden off your shoulders; you're almost there! When putting the hat together, there are two different seaming techniques that you may pick from.

A seam that runs down the sides of the hat may be created by working the last row of stitches through the loops on both the border and the inside.

The very last phase will consist of the seam itself, in addition to the very last row of stitches.

If you choose this option, the outside of the hat will have a barely discernible raised line, although the ribbing texture will help cover it.

Folding the crocheted rectangle in half so that the right sides are visible prepares you to work the last row. Carry out the last row of stitches following the instructions, but this time move your hook through both loops on the first row of work.

To complete the seam, I worked the third row of the pattern (Chain 1, 30 dc in back loop only, four single crochets in back loop only, one single crochet in each of the remaining loops on both sides).

The proper method to create a ribbed hat is by joining the long edges of your crochet hat together to produce a tube shape

Slip stitches are another method that may be used to bind the two sides together. A slip-stitch seam will leave behind a little raised line, which may be turned inside the hat if desired.

Before putting the two halves together, you must crochet the required rows to get the desired length of twenty inches. After that, you must turn the hat so the interior faces outside. A smooth connection may be achieved by working slip stitches (also known as slip stitches) over both loops of thread along both borders.

Gathering the top of the hat is the first step toward crocheting a beanie with pom poms.

As the proverb advises, put on your hat before entering a room.

When you have finished making the last loop, you should draw the yarn through it and then cut off any extra. Using the tail end of the string and a darning needle, so long, zigzag stitches around the edge of the hat.

Using the tail of the yarn, gather the edge of the top of the hat and then pull the drawstring to fasten it. To provide an extra layer of protection, you may knot the end of the yarn. Bring all of the loose ends together.

The finished product is a crocheted winter hat with a folded brim and a flexible ribbing pattern that imitates knit.

Putting a Pom on Your Crochet Hats

My favorite part of crocheting a beanie is when I get to put a fluffy pom on the end of it. They may be made in no time at all, and stitching them into crocheted hats is a piece of cake.

Pom-pom-making tools are reasonably priced, considering what you receive in return, and the finished products are consistently round and flawless. This set is fantastic since it contains all the required components for making pom poms of all sizes, from the tiniest to the largest.

Using a pom-pom maker is one option for making pom-poms; however, various options are available. Fashioning them using one's own hands, a roll of toilet paper, or a cardboard template is possible.

In addition, if you are interested in employing one of those cute pom-poms made of synthetic fur, I have several recommendations.

Included is a little elastic loop that allows for a quick and straightforward connection to any headgear of your choosing.

1.4 EASY CROCHET HAIR SCRUNCHIE – A BEGINNER PATTERN

You will learn how to make charming hair scrunchies by following this free and basic pattern, which is great for beginning crocheters because of its simplicity. It is simple to make scrunchies in the style that was popular in the 1990s, and they would be great to give as gifts or sell at craft festivals. The fact that they can quickly scale up output is an additional perk.

Materials:

Crocheters, Here Are Some Scrunchie-Making Lessons for You

Have you ever given thought to the possibility of creating your hair accessories by hand? This simple design for a hair scrunchie is just what you need to bring a bit of handiwork to your wardrobe.

Someone who is just beginning to learn how to crochet might benefit much from using this pattern. To whip up one of these crochet scrunchies, you only need knowledge of a single fundamental stitch. You will be able to produce one of these scrunchies if you are familiar with the technique of half-double crochet.

Procedure:

These homemade scrunchies have a relatively minimal list of required supplies.

Because just a little ball of yarn is needed for each scrunchie, this pattern is perfect for using yarn remnants.

Gather the items listed below before moving further with the process:

One painless elastic for you to use in your hair. When it comes to my hair, I go for elastic bands that do not include metal crimps since they are solid and long-lasting. If you are just starting with crochet and are afraid about snagging the yarn on a metal hook or tying a knot in it, it is better to simply buy a pack of the "touchless" sort of yarn.

A small hank of yarn with a worsted gauge and a bulky weight. When working with this pattern, I suggest using yarn of worsted weight since it is less difficult to manipulate and results in a fluffy scrunchie in a shorter length. If, on the other hand, you prefer a thinner yarn, DK weight would work just as well; the only thing you'll need to do is adjust the stitch count appropriately.

You will need a crochet hook in size "J," or 6mm, or whatever size is specified by the manufacturer of the yarn you are using.

If you have to sew the two ends together, use a needle for a pretty blunt tapestry.

Instructions for Crocheting Hair Ties as a Pattern

There are many ways to make a crochet scrunchie, and the one you choose will depend on the look you're looking for.

I worked this pattern in the round around an elastic hair tie to have the correct amount of loft and fullness.

If you follow these steps, you can wrap the hair tie in a crochet fabric tube, allowing you to create ruffles with a lot of volumes.

To begin the scrunchie, chain ten stitches and join them together using a slip stitch. OR you may build 10 foundation half double crochets if you already know how to perform that stitch. (Since I like to start with a foundation half double crochet, you will see images of that kind of work.)

After that, make half double crochet stitches around the hair tie to form a tube-shaped piece of fabric using a swirling motion.

Free Crochet Pattern for a Scrunchie to Wear as a Headband or a Scarf

Continue sewing in spiral rows in a clockwise manner after you have your tube of 10 stitches completed.

The first piece of guidance I can provide is to continue crocheting even after the two ends of your tube have been connected. You'll need to create as many rows of HDC as you can if you want to end up with a scrunchie that appears like it was made in the 1990s.

Your ability to manage your hook will become more challenging the more HDC rounds you complete. A completed scrunchie with more games will be more substantial.

When satisfied that the scrunchie has the appropriate volume, you may complete the project by sewing the tube's ends together.

I used 36 rows to tighten my scrunchie, and I think it turned out just right. Depending on the breadth of the hair ties, you may make as many or as few of them as you choose.

Cut your yarn, but make sure to leave a long tail so that you can stitch the scrunchie shut. Utilizing a tapestry needle with a blunt tip, sew the tube's ends together. After that, using the same hand, weave in the ends of the yarn.

If you're worried about your scrunchie coming undone, you may give yourself an extra layer of protection by tying a knot in it. All of those frills will make it difficult for you to see.

And with that, this concludes everything. You may wear an attractive and substantial scrunchie on your wrist or hair. It is yours to keep.

It's a lot of fun to create a batch of these scrunchies, and they make lovely gifts for your loved ones, including your family and friends. They are excellent for whipping up at the eleventh hour as a thoughtful homemade gift because of their ease of preparation.

When you sell these scrunchies at flea markets and craft events, you have the potential to make a significant amount of money. They are not difficult to make and are perennially fashionable.

Instructions

Beginning with ten chains, yarn of worsted weight, and a J crochet hook will get you started. To make a tube, begin by winding the chain around the hair tie and then linking the two ends together using a slip stitch.

You can create 36 rounds of half-double crochet by working in spiral rows. You may need to construct more or fewer rows, depending on the width of the hair tie you're using.

You need to cut the yarn, but you should leave a long tail. You may join the two ends of the tube together using the backside of the thread and a dull tapestry needle. Bring all of the loose ends together.

1.5 CROCHETING A GRANNY SQUARE FOR BEGINNERS

To that end, would you be interested in gaining the skills necessary to crochet a granny square? Creating a granny square may seem complicated, but in reality, all you need is a straightforward crochet method.

Materials:

I will demonstrate how to crochet a granny square by following a pattern I've devised to be easy enough for a beginner to keep in their head. I have included a large number of visual aids as well as thorough instructions for anybody interested in learning how to crochet a conventional granny square.

Granny square worked up in the simplest crochet stitch, the finished product

An enjoyable and straightforward crochet activity is to make a granny square. The granny square is a beautiful pattern if you are beginning to crochet.

The following set of instructions will walk you through the process of crocheting a granny square from the very beginning. Because the pattern is straightforward (and, as a result, specific to memorize), you will have no trouble getting started on your first granny square project immediately.

Procedure:

Once you have a firm grasp on the foundations of granny square crochet, the possibilities are endless in terms of the cozy items you may create with this technique.

Get your favorite hook ready, and we'll start the crocheting immediately. Continue reading if you would like to see the complete tutorial. Continue reading to acquire a written pattern that you can print off for free.

What exactly is meant by the term "granny square"?

In the craft of crochet, a motif often used is a granny square. This item was created using basic crochet stitches such as the chain stitch and the double crochet stitch. One may quickly recognize a granny square by its characteristic square shape and lace-like texture.

Since granny squares are so small, they are an excellent choice for projects that call for the use of scraps of yarn. Create your granny squares using a single color of adventure, or add some variety by switching to a new shade of wool for each round.

A small number of granny squares and some seaming are required to manufacture items like sweaters, Afghans, scarves, and crocheted blankets, just a few examples.

Building Methods and Procedures

The basic pattern for a granny square is made by working in linked rounds, starting in the center and working outward. The way the granny clusters and chains repeat themselves around the court gives the granny court its distinctive appearance.

The pattern known as a granny cluster is created by knitting or crocheting three double crochet (dc) stitches into the same region.

The granny clusters along the sides of the square are separated by chain-1 gaps, while the four corners of the court are divided by chain-3 spaces.

Variations on the theme of the Granny Square

Hundreds of different ways the traditional granny square may be made. It is possible to crochet various granny squares, including traditional granny squares, solid granny squares, solid granny squares with no gaps, sunburst granny squares, and even granny hexagons.

On the other hand, the standard version comprises four rounds of double crochet clusters that are worked into chain gaps. In this tutorial, I'll show you how to make the conventional version yourself.

Creating a Crochet Granny Square in the Traditional Manner

In this tutorial, I'll show you how to crochet a traditional granny square, one of my all-time favorite types of crafts.

Because this pattern is so effective at producing flat granny squares, it is the one I often turn to. By using chain-3 spacing in certain areas, I can prevent rounding off the edges. (Later on, when you're going to sew the grannies together, you won't have nearly as much trouble with it.)

Supplies

You may make a granny square by crocheting with a hook of the appropriate size and using only a tiny amount of yarn.

Regarding the yarn, I'm using a worsted weight for my projects.

I'm currently working with an H-sized crochet hook (5.0mm).

As you knit, a couple of stitch markers will serve as markers at the start of rounds.

For this purpose, you do not need to go out and purchase a whole skein of yarn; instead, you may use a small amount of leftover yarn from your stockpile. Nevertheless, when getting started, I usually advise selecting a thread that is light in color, has a worsted-weight gauge, and has a smooth feel to it. (You'll have an easier time seeing your stitches.) Choose a hook compatible with the needle size that is advised for use with the yarn.

This straightforward granny square will be crocheted by me using just one color. You can work each circle using the same color of yarn or switch to a different color for each one.

Observe and Make Notations on a Pattern

This pattern uses crochet terms that are common in the United States.

After each side of the granny square is individual, the rounds are joined to make the finished square.

Each iteration of this project will have the right-side facing outward.

You will be working into the chain gaps between the stitches of the previous round rather than placing your hook into the threads of the last game.

Stitches are abbreviated as follows:

The granny square is crocheted using a variety of traditional stitches and methods. The pattern's shorthand notation may be found down below.

Stitching in chains, often known as chain stitching

chain space, which is also often referred to as chain stitch-space

The abbreviation "dc" in crochet refers to the "double crochet" stitch.

The use of a needle and thread (Insert hook, yarn over, pull through stitch, and loop on hook)

stitch(es)

Detailed Embroidery Work

The corners of the granny square are constructed using clusters of granny squares linked together using chain spaces.

A granny cluster is a cluster of three double crochet stitches, as the name of the stitch cluster suggests. Chain stitches are utilized in this pattern to provide space between the granny clusters that have been crocheted.

There Are Three Different Ways to Crochet a Granny Square.

There are three different methods to get started on a granny square. Using the magic ring approach, beginning with a single chain stitch, creating a center ring of chain stitches, and starting with a single chain stitch are all valid methods.

To get things started, you may begin in a single file.

Including all of the threads into a single chain stitch with this approach may be challenging, even though it can be learned quickly and with little effort.

Create a chain of three, then put the hook into the top of the first chain to start the first chain stitch in the single chain stitch pattern. On the very first round, you will begin by working the starting chain stitch into each cluster.

Chain stitch may be used to create the center ring as a second option.

Even though it is straightforward and quick, this method produces a wider hole in the center of the square.

One center ring is worked in chain stitch: To finish the circle, you will need to do a slip stitch into the fourth chain that extends from the hook. You are ready to begin the first round when you have finished setting up the circle.

Alternative 3: The Ring of Magical Power (aka Magic Circle)

The magic ring, often known as the magic circle, is the third possible approach. If you follow these steps, you will have a strong core devoid of voids.

If you are unsure how to start your granny square, look at this tutorial for the magic ring.

This tutorial will concentrate on working with the middle ring of a chain stitch, but you are free to substitute any other technique that works best for you.

The Classic Crochet Square, Known as a Granny

The instructions for making a granny square with crochet are provided in text form below.

A Confidence-Inspiring Ring:

Develop the granny square by beginning with a middle ring.

Start by chaining four stitches and inserting your hook into the first chain stitch you make. The chain threads must be connected using a slip stitch to complete the circle.

The first step in making a granny square is to chain four stitches and then join the resulting chains to create a circle.

You will begin Round 1 of the Cluster Crochet patterns by crocheting a single stitch.

Round 1

The first version of the granny square will be explained in great depth further down in this section. The condensed set of instructions may be found further down the page.

Stitching in a chain pattern three qualifies as the first double crochet (dc) stitch in the first granny cluster.

After completing the magic circle, you should work two double crochets into it. If you line up these three DCs in a row, you'll have an idea of what they seem to be like. In this instance, we are dealing with our first cluster of grandmothers. Ch 3.

Start working on the second group of granny squares right away. Within the magic circle, work three rows of double crochet. Ch 3.

Now, in chain 3, knit three double crochets into the center ring of the preceding cluster, and repeat the previous step.

After this, you should construct the fourth grouping. Work three double crochet stitches into the ring in the center. Ch 3.

You should now have four granny clusters and three chain stitches at the corners and the end. Creating a square and connecting the circle is accomplished by working a slip stitch into the third chain worked from the hook. The first period has finally come to an end.

Again, here are the instructions for Round 1, but this time they are presented in the abbreviated version that is most often used:

In the first round, chain 3. In the middle ring, work two double crochets, then a chain stitch 3, followed by three double crochets and another chain stitch 3. This completes one round. Make a slip stitch at the top of the third chain working backward from the hook.

I completed the first square of a granny square pattern by filling it in.

Using a slip stitch join, finish up the first round of knitting.

Round 2:

Chain 4 (at this point, we should be in the first stitch-1 space of both the dc and the chain.)

Work 3 double crochet stitches, three chain stitches, three double crochet stitches, and one chain stitch in the next chain stitch-3 space (also known as the first corner space).

Repeat Step 2 once more, bringing the total number of times it has been done up to three.

In the last chain stitch-3 space, complete the following sequence of stitches: 3 double crochets, three chain stitches, and two double crochets.

Work a slip stitch into the third chain worked from the hook to connect.

The end has come for the second round.

achieving some forward momentum on the second round of a granny square

We will now compete in the next game.

Round 3:

Chain 3. (This counts as one dc.)

In the last step, work two double crochets into the space between the chain stitches and the next round that is directly below. This is a significant step since it is the first granny cluster of this iteration.

In the next corner space between chains, work three double crochets, three chain stitches, three double crochets, and one chain stitch.

In the space created by the previous chain stitch-1, complete the following series of stitches in order: 3 double crochets, then chain stitch 1.

It is necessary to repeat steps 3 and 4 to go back to the beginning of the chain. To complete the project, work a slip stitch into the top of the third chain that was created when the chain was started.

The third iteration of the granny square

The Third Circle of Crochet

Round 4:

Chain 4. (For this, it will need one double crochet and one chain stitch in a space.)

Work three double crochet stitches into the space left by the next chain stitch-1.

Work one chain stitch, three double crochets, three chain stitches, three double crochets, and one chain stitch into the corner area created by the following chain stitch three.

Simply repeat steps 2 and 3 whenever there are any remaining chain stitch-1 and chain stitch-3 holes.

Stitch two double crochets into the space left by the last chain (Ch -1).

Make a slip-stitch connection to the third chain from the beginning of the pattern.

During the fourth and final round, there will be no more action.

A set of instructions for finishing the last game of crocheting a granny square.

On to the Championship Round

Increasing the Size of Granny Squares Through Modification

The total number of granny square rounds determines how large the ultimate product will be. By doing rounds 3 and 4 as often as required, squares of any size may be created via the knitting process.

Pulling the Plug on the Granny Square

After you have finished the final round, you should cut your working yarn, leaving a trail of at least six inches. You will need to bring the thread through to finish the last stitch. Utilizing a blunt yarn needle, weave in the loose ends.

This is it! You have successfully crocheted a granny square in the classic style.

Granny Squares in Several Different Colors

After you've gotten the hang of making granny squares with a single color, you may go on to making ones with several colors.

You may quickly change to a new yarn color by connecting to the next round with a slip stitch when you reach the end of the current one. (If you remember correctly, you will join the games by working a slip stitch into the third chain from the hook when you first start the project.)

1.6 THROW BLANKET IN TRIPLE BERRY CHUNKY CROCHET

Do you need a cuddly, substantial crochet blanket? The textured stripe on this blanket was accomplished with a few simple stitches.

Materials:

Only two stitches—the single and the even berry—are used to create the textured square part of this straightforward pattern for a crochet blanket. This quick and easy chunky throw can be produced quickly using extra-bulky yarn.

The Woven Fabrics

In my next crochet project, I plan to utilize Bernat Blanket Yarn Orgon as my yarn of choice. This is the same yarn used from the beginning; however, it could be drawn using a different technique today.

This Bernat Blanket Yarn has an absurdly high loft and a warm feel despite its low price. Yarn is easily accessible and sells at a price that is not prohibitive.

Procedure:

When it comes to color, you have various choices: blues, pinks, reds, greens, grays, lavender, and many more. There are choices for both single-color and multicolored skeins of yarn. It would be less complicated if you just chose the three standard colors of Bernat Blanket Yarn.

There was a decision made in the design to separate the colors of the yarn; doing so would have suited the purpose for which the thread was meant, but I liked the appearance of entire stripes. There are different skeins of yarn, some of which have a degree of unwinding that is more controllable than others.

Due to its fuzzy texture, this extremely thick yarn might be a little bit of a challenge to work with. Feeling the following accessible stitch location with the hook or your finger is the only way to locate it.

Additional Blanket Crochet Patterns That Are Completely Free to Use

Free pattern for an ombre herringbone crochet blanket or throw.

Instructions in Crochet for Making a Fluffy Blanket

A Free Crochet Blanket Pattern in a Deep Gray Chunky Weight Yarn, Suitable for Use as a Throw on a Couch

Lemonade Pink Chunky Blanket Knitting Pattern

When searching for yarn to construct this crochet blanket pattern, I concluded that Bernat blanket yarn would be the best option—making this blanket won't take very long because of the thick gauge six chenille yarn being used.

Bernat blanket yarn is available in a broad color palette, making it adaptable for usage in various color palettes and patterns.

This chunky triple-berry throw construction may be completed quickly, thanks to the design. A few short stitches produce the pattern's distinctive raised bobbles.

Simply reducing the yarn size is required to make a chunky baby blanket. Because this yarn is made in the chenille manner, it is plush and lofty.

My kid always attempts to hide her face by pulling the blanket over her head.

This chunky crochet throw blanket would be attractive in whatever three colors you choose to work with. If you were to get one of these handcrafted things, it might be beneficial to you as well as a friend or member of your family.

Do you need a substantial number of crocheted blankets made using bulky yarn? Bernat Blanket Yarn contains 35 free blanket designs and 25 crochet blanket patterns.

There are affiliate links on this page. If you click on one of my links and then proceed to make a purchase, I may be eligible to get a commission on the sale at no additional expense to you.

This chunky triple-berry throw construction may be completed quickly, thanks to the design. A few straight stitches produce the pattern's distinctive raised bobbles.

Supplies

Scissors

Needle for tapestry

When crocheting, use a hook size N (9 mm).

Bernat Blanket Orgon Yarn in Winter Berry, weighing between 6 and 10.5 ounces, or any other extra thick yarn with a gauge of 6 (660 yds)

Free crochet pattern for a blanket with large, contrasting stripes.

Acronyms Used in America

crocheting with just one stitch at a time,

a bobble is created by working four rounds of double crochet into the shape of a ball.

The needle and the chain

"Yarn over" is the abbreviation for this phrase.

A pair of stitches created using the half-double crochet technique and done in a herringbone pattern

This is Bobble Stitch: (dc4tog) You, draw up a loop, then pull through both loops while holding the loop you just created. You into that area, draw up a circle, and pull through two loops; repeat twice more; three loops remain on the hook; you and repeat; four loops remain on the theme; you and repeat; five loops stay on the hook; you and pull through all five loops on the hook. We have completed the sewing.

Half double crochet stitch worked in a herringbone pattern: yarn over, insert hook into the next stitch. After that, you will want to drag the working yarn through the stitch and the next loop on the hook. You must thread your finger through the two still circles to complete the theme.

COTTON CROCHET FACE SCRUBBIEST REUSABLE

The notion of crocheting face scrubbiest as a gift is both enjoyable and straightforward. Because they can be recycled and reused, they are an excellent complement to any beauty routine that prioritizes environmental sustainability.

Materials:

Cotton yarn in pink, gold, and white was used to crochet four similar face scrubbers in a circular shape.

Crochet Facecloths and Washcloths for Other Uses

This design of face scrubby is excellent for beginners since it is easy to produce and does not take a lot of time. Check out this pattern for crochet cotton face scrubbiest if you are searching for a quick gift, a winner at a craft fair, or an activity that will help you use little scraps of material.

Procedure:

In my daily hygiene routine, I use these little washcloths instead of makeup wipes that are only good for one use since I manufactured them myself. As a result of the puff stitches, they have a pleasant and spongy texture. Cotton yarn that lasts long absorbs moisture and exfoliates gently to remove dead skin.

They are also quite simple to prepare in a short amount of time. Once the pattern is memorized, it should only take 15 to 20 minutes to complete the face scrubby.

Have you just started crocheting recently? If you are beginning with crochet, you may find it helpful to go back over the essential methods by utilizing my tutorial written just for beginners.

Washable in the machine and reusable.

My mood is brightened because crochet face scrubbiest may be used again after being washed and dried. When you want to clean your face, you may use them instead of cotton balls or a conventional washcloth. Because they are woven from solid cotton yarn, a set of these scrubbers will last you a very long time.

It won't be difficult for you to maintain them alive and in good condition. You may clean them in the same load as the rest of your garments if you choose. They will grow noticeably softer after every wash that you do on them.

An Optimal Approach to the Destruction of Waste Materials

Making one of these scrubbers does not need a significant amount of yarn. It is possible to make many face scrubbers from a single ball of cotton yarn. You may also use any cotton yarn of the worsted weight left over. (Such as these straightforward potholders made of cotton crochet.)

The Ideal Gift for Someone Who Loves to Crochet

You can't go wrong with a set of these crochet face scrubbiest for any occasion, whether it's Mother's Day, a special birthday, Teacher Appreciation Week, or just because. They're perfect for exfoliating your skin and leaving it feeling fresh and clean.

As a kind gift, you might tie a lovely ribbon around a bar of cold-pressed soap and a stack of five scrubbiest and give them to the recipient.

A circular facial scrubber in pink, gold, and white cotton yarn is crocheted with a blue crochet hook. The finished product is a circular scrubby for the face.

Cotton Yarns Have Proven to Be Very Popular

Cotton yarn is my go-to when I'm crocheting items like face washcloths and scrubbiest to use on my face.

Why? Cotton yarn is durable, long-lasting, and can be used several times. It also can absorb moisture. In addition, it may be washed with the rest of your towels in the washing machine and dried in the dryer if you want to.

You don't want to put anything on your sensitive skin that will be too abrasive, so when shopping for cotton yarn, choose a high-quality thread that will feel nice and smooth on your face.

The following are some ideas to consider:

Cotton yarn under Lily Sugar n' Cream has stood the test of time and remains a favorite. It is available in various colors, ranging from solids to stripes to ombre effects, and the color pallet is enormous.

Lion Brand 24/7 cotton may also be used to make easy-care accessories for the kitchen, bathroom, and other rooms in the home. Because the yarn is constructed entirely out of mercerized cotton, it is resilient and shiny.

In conclusion, I recommend working with cotton yarn from Dashier.

Its twist is more tightly wound than conventional cotton yarns, leading to less splitting in the finished product. Additionally, squeezing it is an enjoyable experience. It is also capable of being laundered in a washing machine, in addition to having a significantly extended lifespan.

Many other fiber combinations might work well with this design. Some of such possibilities are: A face scrub that is crafted from a cotton-bamboo yarn seems like it would be a fantastic product, and I'm prepared to bet on that. (Even still, acrylic yarn is not the most excellent option for this undertaking.)

Instructions for Making a Crocheted Face Washcloth as a Pattern

To complete this face scrubber pattern, you will be working in connected rounds in the round. The designer uses American crochet vocabulary throughout the design.

Dossiers de resources

To finish a set of crochet face scrubbers, you will need the following items:

Cotton yarn of the worsted weight sort (CYC 4), such as Lily Sugar n' Cream.

Crochet hook size H (5.0 mm) ((This is one of my favorite hooks that doesn't cost a lot of money.))

a needle that is often used in darning or tapestry

Measurements

After being finished, the circle has a radius of 3.75 inches around it. You can change the size of the scrubby by either adding or subtracting rounds while keeping the pattern that was set.

Gauge

It is not a deal-breaker for this endeavor if the measurements are off-target.

To crochet a face scrubby with the exact dimensions as mine, you will need cotton yarn of worsted weight and a crochet hook with an H-size.

Cotton yarn in pink, gold, and white was used to crochet four similar face scrubbers in a circular shape.

Stitches are abbreviated as "stitches."

Their explanations are provided below if you encounter any stitch abbreviations in the pattern.

Stich is short for chain stitch (s)

The term "puff" refers to the following construction: a puff stitch followed by a single chain.

Single crochet is always worked in the same manner.

indistinguishable from a slip stitch

stitches are equal to stitches (es)

Detailed Embroidery Work

The second and third rounds of the crochet scrubby are made using a special "puff stitch." The specifics of this stitch will be outlined in the text after this one.

An Instructional Guide on Crocheting the Puff Stitch

This hook has nine strands attached to it.

a technique for closing off a puff stitch with an extra chain

It seemed like there was an extra chain stitch.

Method of Stitching: Puff followed by Chain 1

It's likely not news to you that there are many different puff stitches to choose from. The sizes of the various instances are somewhat variable. Some patterns call for an extra chain stitch to be worked to finish off the puff, while others do not.

The puff stitch, which has nine loops on the hook at the end, is used to construct this pattern. Additionally, the closure for this stitch is a final chain 1, which is the case.

A yarn over is followed by the insertion of the hook into the next stitch, and then a loop is drawn tight (3 loops on the theme)

After that, insert the hook into the stitch, yarn over, and make a loop through the newly created hole (5 loops on the theme)

To make a loop, you need to do a yarn over three times, insert your hook, and pull through the stitches (7 loops on the theme)

After working the previous stitch, insert the hook through it, do a yarn over four times, and pull up a loop (9 loops on the theme)

To complete this step, you will need to yarn over and pull through each of the nine loops on the hook.

Acquire one chain starting from the very beginning.

Make a ring of power as your initial step.

Ten single crochet stitches are worked into the magic ring to complete the first round. You may terminate the circle by working a slip stitch over the top of the initial single crochet stitch. This will allow you to link the stitches together. The repair only ten stitches to complete.

To begin crocheting a circle of scrubbiest, you must first make a magic ring.

Chain 2 for the second round (does not count as a stitch). Create a puff stitch with the same thread and continue doing so all the way around. Joining the circle is accomplished by working a slip stitch into the first puff stitch (20 stitches).

If the fact that I have 20 stitches after round 2 gives you a hard time, remember that I add an extra chain 1 to the end of each puff stitch. This should clear things up for you. So far, I've completed ten chain stitches and ten puff stitches. Here we go!

Directions for continuing to crochet a cotton face scrubby that may be used in either direction

Chain 2 for the third round (does not count as a stitch). Perform a puff stitch in the space between the next stitch and the chain stitches all the way around. You may complete the circle by working a slip stitch into the first puff stitch. This will allow you to link the stitches. (A total of forty stitches)

Chain 1 for the fourth round (does not count as a stitch). Single crochet in the stitch before the final stitch and in each surrounding stitch. (32) Make a slip knot in the first single crochet stitch to complete the circle. (Seventy-five stitches)

Cut off any extra yarn, secure it with a knot and weave in the ends.

Directions for the third round of the puff stitch in a cotton crochet scrubby.

A hook for hanging things is not required.

If you want to dry the scrubby more quickly, you may connect a loop to it and then hang it from a hook. This will help you save time.

If you wish to make a loop, don't finish off at the end of the fourth circle, where you would typically do so. Create a loop by working a slip stitch back into the last stitch of the fourth round.

Rather than doing this, make a chain sequence roughly three inches long and then perform the slip stitch into the previous thread of the chain sequence. Bring all the loose ends together and tie them off.

How to Make the Most of Your Facial Scrubs

Scrubbiest are an alternative to a regular washcloth and may be used in its stead. Fill the scouring sponge up with water and squeeze as much as you can out of it. Put some facial cleanser or soap in the sink, and then begin cleaning your face.

Scrubs may be washed using conventional methods by first being placed in a lingerie bag or a mesh laundry bag and then put through the washing machine.

CROCHET PATTERN FOR A SOLID GRANNY SQUARE

Following my instructions, please find out how to make a modern and robust granny square. You'll learn how to crochet your beautiful granny squares using just the simplest skills by following these images, which are both straightforward and to the point.

Materials:

There are a great many projects that may benefit from using granny squares. Construct a classic granny square, or try your hand at one of the many other potential variants.

The solid granny square is a popular variation of the pattern. It is possible to crochet granny squares with either open corners or without any gaps at all.

Procedure:

My go-to pattern for making solid granny squares with open corners is this one, which I've tried quite a few variations over the years.

Typical placement for turning chain stitches in a pattern is along the middle of one of the sides. That is efficient, although the "seam" of the twisting chain could be uncomfortable to the viewer.

You may have worked with a design that requires a turning chain of five chains, with the understanding that three chains count as one double crochet and the remaining two chains generate the chain stitch-2-space. While I enjoy the arrangement, I can't help but note that one of the four corner spots is much larger than the others.

I was ecstatic to learn a brand-new method for knitting a solid granny square on Pinterest, courtesy of Irishlace.net. The process is quite simple.

chart for the first two rounds of a granny square for a solid and seamless square

It is practical since the turning chain is located near the corner chain stitch-2-space, albeit not directly next to it. By doing it this way, the "seam" will be concealed, and the proportions of the four apertures in the corner will stay the same.

If you would instead not utilize crochet charts, the directions are written out for you in straightforward English.

Squares worked in crochet with a solid pattern.

Level of Difficulty: Easy to Start With

Regarding the gauge, its inclusion in this design is not required to succeed. The size of the crochet hook you use should be adjusted appropriately for the weight of the yarn.

The finished product should have a square measurement of 5 inches when working with worsted-weight yarn and a hook of size H.

Hook: H (5.0 mm)

Worsted-weight yarn is used in weaving (Category 4)

Additional materials consist of the following:

Needle for yarn

stitch indicators that are unnecessary to use

If you like, you may use a gauge; otherwise, a tape measure will serve.

A Selection of Acronyms and Abbreviations

stitches: stitch(es) stitch(es) (es)

"chain" or "chain stitch," respectively.

chain-2-space, also known as chain stitch-2-space (which will be the corner space)

The acronym for double stitches in crochet work.

Sewing errors, stitching errors

A Few Notes Regarding the Pattern:

The pattern makes use of words that are widespread in the United States. These phrases are utilized in the design.

Every chain stitch that is worked at the beginning of a round counts as one stitch unless specified differently in the pattern.

I am going to work one double crochet into the first three chains. If you find that this stitch is too loose for you, please try chain stitch 2.

A bigger or smaller granny square will arise, depending on whether or not further rounds are added similarly.

After chaining five stitches to build a foundation ring, complete the connection with a slip stitch. Alternatively, you might use the technique of the magic ring.

The magic ring approach is a great way to start a granny square that will last.

Round 1:

Chain 3. (Work this into the pattern at any point to represent double crochet.)

Double crochet one stitch into the ring, then double crochet twice into the chain immediately after that.

Repeat these stitches within the circle three times (3 dc, two chain stitches).

One double crochet should be worked into the foundation chain and linked to the top of the chain using a slip stitch. [12 stitches, four chain spaces, and two stitch spaces]

When working a chain stitch, be sure to insert another slip stitch into the second slot (corner space)

A whole granny square worked in rounds one and two

Round 2:

Chain 3. (This counts as one dc.)

Work 1 double crochet, two chain stitches, and two double crochets into the space provided to complete the next corner.

Performing one double crochet in each side dc and two double crochets in the corner chain stitch-2 gap are the instructions for this pattern. Carry on in the same manner for the subsequent two faces.

Complete the last remaining side by working a dc into the dc space. Do one double-crochet of the top of the slip stitch from the previous round. It is recommended that one double crochet be worked into the slip stitch of the game that follows (the one that went into the corner space.) Continue working in slip stitches until you reach the very top of the foundation chain. [28 stitches, with two spaces between stitches in four chains]

When working a chain stitch, be sure to insert another slip stitch into the second slot (corner space)

describing how to begin crocheting a solid granny square using a double crochet stitch

Check to see whether you are skipping the first dc stitch on each side if you are having difficulties counting your stitches. This might be causing the problem. Other stitches you work into the corner region may sometimes hide this stitch. As a result, you will need to untie the corner threads to identify the first stitch on each side.

a set of instructions for constructing a robust granny square

The last double crochet stitch of the round must be worked into the slip stitch of the competition before it.

By repeating this pattern as often as you want, you may create your granny square, whatever size you choose.

The pattern you worked on in Round 2 will be repeated in Round 3 [44 stitches, four chains stitch-2 spaces].

For the fourth and final round, repeat Round 2's stitch count and gap pattern (60 stitches, four chain stitches, two gaps).

[76 stitches, four chain stitches, and two spaces] for the fifth round. It's time for Round 2!

Work the same pattern as Round 2 (92 stitches, four chains stitch-2 spaces) to complete the sixth round.

Work the same as you did in Round 2 for the seventh round (108 stitches, four chain stitch-2 gaps).

Cut the yarn, secure the end, and weave in the ends of your granny square when it has achieved the appropriate size. If, after getting started, there is still a gap in the center, you may use the tail to fill it in.

This is it! You've just completed crocheting a square. Congratulations!

CHILDREN'S CROCHET HEART PATTERN

This Valentine's Day, put your crocheting skills to the test by making one of these adorable hearts. The cutest is a crochet heart garland from these charming and squishy little hearts.

Materials:

If you are looking for a thoughtful handmade gift that you can make in a short time for Valentine's Day (or any other day of the year) to show how much you care about someone, this crochet heart pattern is the one for you.

a magnified portion of an image showing a crocheted heart in detail

Crochet Patterns for Easy-to-Make Hearts

These crochet hearts are the perfect option, whether you're searching for a gift that you can make yourself or some festive décor for Valentine's Day. They are capable of performing such a wide variety of functions!

Procedure:

Make adorable appliques out of them and sew them onto baby sweaters or tote bags for a decorative touch. Simply tying the hearts together is all required to make a crochet heart garland. You may also crochet some coasters out of cotton yarn and use them if you want to do something different for Valentine's Day.

You may find a multitude of more crochet designs in the form of hearts on this page: 14 different patterns for crocheted Valentine's Day hearts

Building Blocks for a Mellow Heart

This heart is best suited for more experienced crocheters since the design calls for increases and a wide variety of crochet stitches (including single, half-double, double, treble, and slip stitches). Crochet stitches are worked in rounds around a magic ring to create the heart design.

If you do not have the worsted-weight yarn on hand, you may easily change the pattern so that it will work with wool of different weights. It is essential to use the appropriate size crochet hook.

There are Three Size Variations Available for the Pattern.

Three distinct possibilities for the size of the hearts may be created using the heart pattern. You will have the shape of a soul after you are through with the first round of crocheting. If you stop after Round 2, you'll have a heart that's about as big as a medium, and if you stop after Round 3, you'll have a crochet heart that's almost as big as a large.

The size of the heart may also be adjusted depending on whether you use thicker or thinner yarns.

Filling for the Crochet Heart, Optional

A puffy heart is created by sewing together two regular seats and stuffing each of the resulting pockets with polypill.

Seven crocheted hearts were produced by using pink yarns in the process.

The Pattern for Crocheting a Heart

I highly doubt that I am the first person to develop a crochet heart pattern, nor will I ever be the last to do so. However, the design in the form of a heart that I will share with you today is my favorite.

In the following paragraphs, you will find detailed instructions for crocheting a heart.

The level of difficulty ranges from upper-level novice to middle-level intermediate.

Your completed work should have dimensions of 3.25 inches across and 3 inches in height when worked with yarn of worsted weight and a hook of 5.0 mm.

This design works effectively with a wide variety of gauges. On the other hand, when I crochet with yarn, I often use a hook one or two sizes smaller than the one that is advised for use with the rope. The hearts appear more determined when prepared in this fashion (without gaps between stitches).

You can make hearts of whatever size you choose by altering the quantity of yarn you use and the size of the crochet hook you use.

The colorway I picked, Lion Brand Mandala Ombre in Felicity, is an example of the Worsted-weight yarn.

Hook size: H (5.0 mm)

Additional materials consist of the following:

Needle for yarn

stitch indicators that are unnecessary to use

scissors

Various Symbols, as well as Stitches

stitches, stitches, and more stitches

Chain stitching is also known as chain stitching.

crocheting with just one stitch at a time

a pair of stitches worked in half double crochet

The abbreviation "dc" in crochet refers to the "double crochet" stitch.

A kind of crochet stitch known as "trebles."

Terminology related to stitching: slip stitch

Observe and Make Notations on a Pattern

The design utilizes the language of the United States of America as its primary language choice.

The cardiovascular system benefits greatly from repeated bouts of exercise.

The Process of Creating a Pattern

As a point of departure, you should use a ring of power. Should you find that you have forgotten the fundamentals of this strategy.

The first chain will consist of two. Create three triple crochets, four double crochets, three triple crochets, and four double crochets, and put them into the ring. Stitch with a slip stitch within the magic ring, then chain two stitches.

She was putting the first crochet round on the heart and getting it started.

This marks the beginning and finish of the first round of stitching.

Simply pull the tail of the yarn to close the magic ring.

If all you wish to do is crochet a few little hearts, you may now reach the point where you can quit.

a heart made by crocheting after the first round has been completed

One that is round and of the closed-magic-ring style

By continuing to work in linked rounds and putting your hook into the stitches from the previous game, you will finish the second round of the project.

Sc in the next space created by chain two, work (2 dc and one dc) in the next stitch, three dc in the next stitch, two dc in the next stitch, dc in the next four stitches (dc, tr, dc) in the next stitch, dc in the next four stitches, two dc in the next stitch, three dc in the next stitch, one dc and two dc in the next stitch

What kind of space is available for a chain with a stitch-2? The second round starts with you working into the area produced by your initial chain stitch of the round, which is a chain-2 space.

Proceed in the same manner, and conclude the round by closing the chain-2 gap you established when the previous game ended. These two vacant chain spaces are adjacent to treble crochet stitches on both sides.

Please note that this is the point at which you should cease forming a little heart.

finishing up the second section of a crochet heart

The third and final rotation of the round-robin exercise.

Single crochet stitches are worked into the first two stitches of the pattern. Single crochet, half double crochet, and single crochet stitches are worked into the next stitch. Single crochet stitches are worked into the next six stitches, followed by three repetitions of one single crochet followed by two single crochet stitches.

To make a seam that is not visible, weave the ends of the yarn into the project. Pull the magic ring tighter, and then hide the stops to make it even more secure.

Continuing a heart motif from the previous round into the third round of crocheting

Finishing

In the third and final round of the heart design, I like to use an invisible join rather than a slip-stitch join. This is because an invisible join is almost undetectable. It is possible to create the look of a stitch by employing a join that cannot be seen.

To establish a smooth connection:

Cut the yarn at that point if you wish to leave a tail that is six inches long.

You will need to bring the yarn through to finish the last stitch. To begin, thread the end of the rope through a tapestry needle.

Insert the needle through the tops of the first stitch worked in the round before this one. However, you should ensure it is a good fit without overdoing it by tugging too firmly.

The top of the last stitch you worked on in the round before this one will serve as the location for your next stitch. Pass the needle through the gap created by the two top loops. By drawing the yarn closer, you can guarantee that the invisible join will be the same size as the stitches surrounding it.

After that, the ends may be sewn in as average.

HEADBAND WITH TWISTED CROCHET EAR WARMERS

This guide will teach you how to crochet a cute and cozy twist-front ear warmer headband in a knit-like stitch pattern. This headband will keep your ears warm and look knit. This crochet headband pattern can serve both a decorative and functional purpose is one of the reasons I like it so much. During the winter, the bulky yarn will prevent the cold from reaching your ears and keep them warm.

A crocheted headband that has the appearance of knitted stitches and a twisted front.

Materials:

A Unique Ear Warmer Crafted with Crochet

I like crocheting headbands so that I may wear something around my head to keep my ears warm. They look well with various hairstyles, from neat buns to messy ponytails and everything in between.

The twist in front may seem harsh, but believe me when I say it's not. Knitting takes place in rows on a flat surface to create a genuine headband. It only has one seam in the shape of a loop. The actual seam is deceptively straightforward, but its design makes it seem as if there is a twist.

This ribbing method is fantastic because, even though it seems to be knitted ribbing, it is constructed by crocheting single stitches and slip stitches.

Procedure:

In other words, if you know how to crochet a rectangle, you already have the skills to make this ear warmer. Now that we've gotten that out of the way let's get to work.

A novel approach to the crocheted headband is shown here.

Pattern for a Crochet Headband with a Twisted Front to Work in Double Crochet Stitches

Incredibly Straightforward

Twenty-one inches in diameter after it is finished.

Adding or deleting the first set of links is all required to make the circumference adjustments. Additional information may be found in the "Sizing Notes" section.

We advise using the Color Made Easy Yarn from Lion Brand for this project.

The weight of the yarn is Category 5, which indicates that it is rather substantial.

K-10.5 Size Hook (6.5 mm)

You should have 12 stitches and 15 rows for every inch when utilizing the pattern stitch.

The Other Thing (or Things) That You Will Need

A tapestry needle with a large eye was used to stitch the seam.

Stitch indicators that are unnecessary to use

If you like, you may use a gauge; otherwise, a tape measure will serve.

You should stitch the ear warmer together using a needle and some thread.

Abbreviations and Terms Used When Knitting or Crocheting Using the Knit and Purl Stitches

This pattern makes extensive use of US crochet phrases throughout.

Back loop only (back loop only) This stitch is worked by inserting your crochet hook beneath the back loop and completing the remainder of the pattern as advised.

"chain" or "chain stitch," respectively.

The most elementary form of crochet, which also happens to be the world's most basic form

sewing errors, stitching errors

stitches: stitch(es) stitch(es) (es)

Observe and Make Notations on a Pattern

When knitting in rows, the turning chain is not counted as a stitch in any of the rows.

If you want the head to be larger or smaller, you must adjust the number of chains you put into Row 1 at the beginning of the pattern.

Notes Regarding the Sizing

To account for the flexibility of the crochet material, the headband you make should have a diameter that is between one and two inches smaller than the circumference of your head.

If you were knitting this headband for a middle-sized adult with a head circumference of 22 inches, you would chain a sufficient number of stitches for the ear warmer to measure 21 inches.

In the following table, you'll discover the finished dimensions of the ear warmers.

A child would need a size 17-inch chain with 52 links.

Eighteen inches in length, with a link chain of 55 inches. Suitable for a child.

Twenty inches in length with 61 links of chain for the XS/S size.

A chain that is 21 inches long and has 64 links is considered the average size for an adult.

The chain is 22 inches long and has 67 links for adults—size L.

Please keep in mind that the length of this headband does not have the same degree of elasticity as, for instance, the brim of a beanie that has been crocheted.

Because of this, you won't be seeking the same level of pain. (The difference between the final headband size and the head size is referred to as having "negative ease," and it is being described here using that phrase.)

I am putting together a headband via crocheting.

Row 1: Ch 64 (the number of chains determined in the size chart above). Using a single crochet stitch, work into the second chain from the hook and each chain across. Turn a chain one spin. (63)

Work a slip stitch across the back loop of the stitch and the back loop of the following stitch on Row 2. Start by chaining one and making a turn. (63)

Across the third row, you'll be working only in the back loop of the stitches. Turn a chain one spin. (63)

To create a headband with a width of 4 inches, you will need to repeat Rows 2 and 3 15 times and then end with a row of single crochet.

Complete the yarn project, but leave a long tail for seaming.

Finishing

The headband must be positioned so that the "right side" faces up when it is put down flat. When you have the right sides of the headband touching, make a tidy fold along the length of the headband.

Hold in each hand one of the short-folded ends of the piece. Raise the two folded sides that overlap and bring them together in the center.

The unfinished edges of the headband were folded over in preparation for the seaming.

Fold each half in half again and overlap them, then place one side into the other. In this particular instance, kindly refer to the picture that is located above. Imagine for a moment two "C" shapes that interlock at opposing ends and create a single structure.

To Produce a Seam, You Will Need to:

For the needle to get through, there must be four layers. Join the two sides by threading a tapestry needle through the end of the yarn. Once the twist is in place, the seam will be hidden entirely from view at all times.

Finish off the look by tucking the tails in and turning the headband inside out.

CROCHET CAN MAKE CHILDREN COZY

Learning to crochet a cozy can allows you to keep your drinks at the perfect temperature and your surfaces dry.

The pattern for creating a can cozy out of cotton yarn is given here for free, and it's straightforward to follow. In addition, I'll show you how to adapt the pattern for this quick and easy crochet cozy so that it works with cans that have a thin or narrow profile. This will allow the comfortable to accommodate more cans.

Materials:

Crocheted can cover made of cotton yarn, shown from the top.

Can cozies, often referred to as koozies are enjoyable crochet projects that can be completed in less than an hour. Obtain some to ensure your beverage stays ice cold as you bask in the warm sun by the lake or beach.

Have you just started crocheting recently? Before going on to the more advanced 6 Easy Crochet Stitches, you should get some practice with this beginner-friendly How to Crochet guide first.

A Few of the Many Reasons Why I Adore This Structure

It's a great way to use leftover yarn scraps if you crochet can holders and wrap them in cozy blankets. You may create them using as few or as many colors as you choose, along with a reasonable amount of cotton yarn. You are free to wear them in their original form or be creative by adding your colors and designs.

Procedure:

You are welcome to use this pattern to produce things you may use to adorn your house, give as gifts to your hostess, or sell at craft fairs.

They are also excellent options for presents to give your dad on Father's Day. A great gift may be made much better by adding a case of beer in a six-pack format. If you want to show your support for your favorite team, you can even have them manufactured in their colors.

Moss Stitch in a Round Routine

The moss stitch in crochet, also referred to as the linen stitch and the granite stitch, creates a lovely texture, and I like working with it. It is a little bit confusing.

The moss stitch produces a lovely surface pattern while being relatively straightforward to execute. To me, it looks almost exactly how a woven material would.

Work in rows of alternating chains and single crochet to create the moss stitch, which is worked in crochet.

Working moss stitch in rows on a flat surface is an essential process; however, working moss stitch in the round may initially provide some difficulties.

Create a foundation chain consisting of an even number of stitches, then use a slip stitch to connect the individual threads. (As you can see below, chains or single crochet may serve as foundation stitches for your project.)

Afterward, you will make a chain of two stitches and work a single crochet stitch into the second chain from the hook.

Beyond that, work a single crochet stitch into the next stitch, skipping the one after that. Proceed in the same sequence until the end of the round has been reached. As the very final stitch in the circle, you should do a single crochet stitch.

To complete the circle, insert a slip stitch into the space between the chains you made at the beginning of the round.

Chain 1 to start the second round of the pattern. Hook the yarn into the first gap left by chain 1, then skip the next stitch and chain 1. Proceed in the same sequence until the end of the round has been reached. A single chain stitch at the end of the competition is the correct technique to complete a game.

To link the rounds, make a slip stitch into the first single crochet of the game.

Two crocheted can cozies are shown next to one another here.

Cotton yarn is my go-to for projects of this kind because of its long-lasting quality and capacity to absorb moisture. You can also use any worsted-weight thread of your choosing, whether it is made of acrylic or any other fiber.

Cotton yarn of worsted weight, also known as CYC 4, is suggested, and excellent examples include companies like Lily Sugar's Cream.

Crochet hook size 5 mm (H)

either a darning needle or a tapestry needle

AB equals the colors A and B;

the meaning of the word "chain" as it appears in "chain stitch."

"Stitch in the round" is synonymous with "stitch in the round."

the addition of one or more stitches;

Anything that follows the * will be repeated, given that * = repeat.

Indicated.

Measurements

The width of the blanket is 7.5 centimeters (3 inches), and its height is 10 centimeters (2.5 inches) (10 cm).

Because cotton yarn tends to stretch with use, the cozy may first seem as if it is too tight.

A Convenient Variation on the Standard Slim Can

After finishing row 4, complete the bottom circle to make a can cozy, that is suitable for a can that is thin or narrow (24 stitches). After this, you should go to the sides of the container and repeat the operation there.

Gauge

Throughout the knitting operation, it is necessary to keep the ideal gauge to forestall the cozy from slipping off the container. Measurement of the bottom circle is what I find most helpful in verifying the meter.

1-5 Rounds Equals 3 Inches (7.5 cm). Any size hook will provide the desired gauge when appropriately used.

Similarly, if your linen stitch is coming out too tight, you may always try a bigger hook size to see if that helps.

Can cozies crocheted using the moss pattern and available in two different ombre colors

The design makes use of American jargon and vocabulary throughout.

Knitted or crocheted in the round using connected rounds, the can cozy is worked in the game.

This phrase is used at the beginning of each round to ensure that the initial chain one does not count as a stitch.

When not in use, the yarns of the garment's primary color (A) and its contrast color (B) should be kept together and stashed along the inside of the garment.

You have to get to the very last loops on the hook that were used for the previous color before you may switch colors. To change colors, yarn over and pull through the remaining loops on the crochet hook. The next thing to do is to take advantage of the new color. (Transitioning from one color to the next will be complete when you reach the slip stitch join.)

Pattern

Construct a Magic Circle with the hue that will serve as the focal point (A). Read this instruction manual to learn how to create your magic circle.

Create a magic circle and put six single crochet stitches into it for the first round. By pushing on the loop, it is possible to make the circle somewhat less expansive. Slip stitches are used to join the initial single crochet to the row.

Beginning with chain 1, work a single crochet stitch in each stitch around. Work a slip stitch into the top of the first single crochet to connect.

steps for crocheting a whole circle using a single crochet stitch

In the third round, you will start with a chain one, single crochet in the first stitch, two single crochet in the next stitch, *single crochet in the next stitch, two single crochets in the next stitch; repeat from * around, and then join with a slip stitch in the first single crochet.

Fourth round: chain 1, two single crochets in the first stitch, single crochet in each of the next two stitches, *two single crochets in the next stitch, chain 1.

Single crochet in each of the next two stitches; repeat from * all the way around. You will need a slip stitch to attach the yarn in the first single crochet.

Adjustment for a skinny can: Join this row to the bottom circle to make a can that is thin or slender (24 stitches). After completing the top, you may work on the sides (skip row 5 and continue with row 6).

Regarding the fifth round: chain one, single crochet in the first three stitches, two single crochets in the next stitch, *single crochet in the next three stitches, two single crochets in the next stitch;

Repeat the iteration that starts with * and ends with * again. To connect, work a slip stitch into the very first stitch.

In Round 6, work single crochet into each stitch around, focusing just on the back loops of the stitches. Slip together to form a whole.

The first stitch is performed in a stitch

Creating a snug circle with crochet might do the trick.

Start working on the moss stitch (the linen or granite stitch).

The seventh round is carried out in the following manner: chain 2, skip the first stitch, single crochet in the next stitch, *chain stitch. Repeat from * until there are no stitches left. After missing the next stitch, a single crochet stitch is worked into the following stitch; *repeat from * all the way around. It is OK to finish your project with a single crochet stitch if that is how you did it. You will need to use a slip stitch to insert your hook into the space you created in the chain at the beginning of the round.

Chain one, single crochet in the first chain stitch-1 spaces, chain one, skip the next stitch, *single crochet in the next chain stitch-1 space, chain one, skip the next stitch; repeat from * around. This completes the eighth round. The right way to complete the project is to chain 1. To attach the pieces, work a slip stitch into the first single crochet stitch.

It is possible to crochet a cozy can using the moss stitch in a circular configuration.

9-14th stanza. Keep on with the primary color for Rounds 7 and 8; after Round 14, you should switch to the contrast color (B).

I crocheted a can of cozies using two colors of cotton yarn to create the pattern.

The seventh round is repeated in the fifteenth, although this time with a different hue (B).

For the sixteenth round, the primary color should again be used as the accent color (A).

For Round 17, you will need to repeat Row 7 using a contrasting color (B).

Work in the primary color for Round 18, just like you did in Round 8. (A).

Rows 7 and 8 should be repeated for Rows 19-21 while utilizing the contrasting color (B).

To make two can cozy, you need a crochet needle and yarn in an ombre pattern.

Finishing

Adjust the screw tension. Use a weave to connect any loose ends.

COTTON SWIMSUIT FOR WOMEN
Materials:

It is necessary to have either 246 yards (225 meters) of faded yarn or 492 yards (450 meters) of another worsted weight, category four yarn, to complete the Lion Brand Jeans, 1 (2, 2) skein, and Color A pattern.

To get color B, you will need 1 (1, 2) skein of Lion Brand Jeans in Stonewash or about 246 yards/225 meters (492 yards/450 meters) of another worsted weight, category four yarn.

Approximately 246 yards / 225 meters (492 yards / 450 meters, 492 yards / 450 meters) of Lion Brand Jeans in Classic or a comparable worsted weight, category four yarn for color C. 1 (2, 2) skeins.

1 (2, 2) skeins of color D using about 246 yards (225 meters) of Lion Brand Jeans in Brand New or 492 yards (450 meters) of another worsted weight, category four yarn.

Crochet hook, US size L/11 (8mm)

Needles for tapestry

STATE IN WHICH IT IS FINISHED:

S/M: 21" (53cm), M/L: 26.5" (67cm), L/XL: 32" (81cm), XXL/XXXL: 32" (81cm).

The length of the garment is 30 inches (or 76 centimeters) for sizes small all the way up to x-large, while it is 32 inches (or 81 centimeters) for sizes two and three times that size.

GAUGE:

To acquire 10cm/4 ", 11 stitches are required for the width when using the half double crochet stitch, and 8.75 rows are needed.

The instructions for the Two of Wands are only available in the English language.

"chain" in its slang form.

Double crochet is what "dc" refers to in crochet lingo.

Abbreviation for half double crochet: hc (half double crochet)

Another "Rep" is due, so let's get to it.

When referring to the right side, the acronym RS should be used.

A single stitch is performed in crochet.

In other words, you are free to ignore it completely.

S.P. is an abbreviation that stands for "space."

"St(s)" is short for "stitch" (es)

Procedure:

Take notice that the garment is created from three independent sections, each seamed together to form the finished product. When counting rows worked in half-double crochet, skip the chain-2 gap at the beginning of each row. The last yarn over the row before should be operated in the new color to indicate a color change. It is important to remember that this pattern is designed for three different sizes (S/M, L/XL, and XXL/XXL), and it must be worked according to the guidelines for the size currently being worked on.

Two Primary Sections:

One hundred sixty-seven chains in chain stitch, using color A. (167, 176).

Half double crochet stitches are worked over the whole row, beginning at the third chain from the hook. (The total number of stitches is 165, 165, and 174)

Two chains, then half double crochet in each of the following rows (RS): (7, 9).

Proceed to color B after you have finished.

Single crochet stitches should be worked across rows 6 and 8, and a chain one turn should be performed across row 10.

The following constitutes the pattern for Row 7 (9, 11): chain 5 (counts as one dc and a chain stitch-2 gap), skip two stitches, dc in next stitch, *chain stitch 2, skip two stitches, dc in next stitch, rep from * till the end of row (chain five counts as one dc and a chain stitch-2 gap).

You will start the remaining portions of Rows 8 and 10 by chaining 1, and then you will work the following pattern: *single crochet 1, single crochet two into the next position between the chains*, and then you will continue from * to the end of the row.

Toggle to the C-shade position.

I am using the chain two technique, completing three rows of half double crochet over rows.

Proceed to color B after you have finished.

Row 14 is done with a single crochet stitch throughout (18, 22).

The following constitutes the pattern for Row 15 (19, 23): Chain 5 (this counts as one double crochet and a chain stitch-2 gap), skip two stitches, dc in the next stitch, *chain stitch 2, skip two stitches, dc in the next stitch, rep from * till the end of the row.

Chain 1, single crochet into the first chain space, single crochet into the second chain space, repeat from * until the end of row (16). (20, 24). To adjust the shade, choose D.

Using the foundation chain, work half double crochet over rows 17-21, then rows 21-27 and 25-33.

A little bit in the center of the back:

According to the design, there should be 85 chains in color D. (85, 91).

Work single crochet stitches across Row 1 (RS), beginning in the second chain from the hook. You will need to do this three times to end up with 90 stitches.

Chain 5 (this counts as one double crochet and the space formed by two chains), skip two stitches, dc in the next stitch, *chain 2, skip two stitches, dc in the next stitch, repeat from * to the end of the row. This completes the second row.

Ch 5 (counts as one dc and chain stitch-2 space), skip one dc and chain stitch-2 space, dc in next dc, *chain stitch 2, SK chain stitch-2 space, dc in next dc, rep from * with final dc going into the 2nd chain stitch of the turning chain stitch from the previous row. Rows 3 and 4: Repeat Rows 2 and 3, but instead of chain

Beginning with the fifth row, chain one and then do the following sequence: *single crochet 1, single crochet two into the next spot in the chain, and repeat from * until the row is complete.

Consider the situation as a whole.

The Arverne Beach Robe, designed by Two of Wands, is an excellent option for wearing when relaxing on the beach.

The Arverne Beach Robe, designed by Two of Wands, is an excellent option for wearing when relaxing on the beach.

Construction:

After that, flip the three pieces so that the right sides are facing out, and then sew the center back panel to the two main panels, starting at the bottom. Do this while the right sides are facing out.

Armholes and vents should have a gap of around 8 inches/20 centimeters at the bottom, approximately 9 inches/23 centimeters at the shoulder seam, and about 7 inches/18 centimeters at the top.

The Arverne Beach Robe, designed by Two of Wands, is an excellent option for wearing when relaxing on the beach.

Collar:

With the right side facing up, join color B at the right center front edge, about 4 inches (10 cm) above the hem.

Work single crochet in the first row in an even pattern across the right front, the back neckline, and down the left front. Stop working on the left side 4 inches (10 cm) before the hem.

Chain 5 (this counts as one double crochet and the space formed by two chains), skip two stitches, dc in the next stitch, *chain 2, skip two stitches, dc in the next stitch, repeat from * to the end of the row. This completes the second row.

Chain five, turn, slip stitch twice into the next chain stitch-2 space, slip stitch into the next dc, slip stitch twice into the next chain stitch-2 space, slip stitch into the next dc, chain two, skip two stitches, dc in the next stitch, *chain two, skip two stitches, dc in the next stitch, rep from * across the row. This will ensure that the collar is even on both sides.

Belt:

To create a chain in color B with 211 stitches: (221, 231). Begin making a row of single crochets, starting from the chain two chains away from the hook.

To make the tassels, cut four lengths of color C measuring 18 inches (46 centimeters) each and forty measurements of color C measuring 12 inches (30.5 centimeters). Cut each of the 40 pieces 12 inches (30.5 cm) long in half so that they are each now 20 pieces. Use any 18 "/46-centimeter components, then tie a knot in the middle of each bundle. Every bundle must be folded in half lengthwise, with the knot placed at the end of the resulting loop.

Wrap the remaining 18 in saran wrap "/ 46-centimeter lengths in a cross pattern around each folded bundle, stopping roughly half an inch or 1.25 centimeters below the top of the fold. After that, thread the tails of the ties inside and down the center of the bundles using a tapestry needle.

At the end of each belt strap, tie a knot and connect the tassels to that. Please use a tapestry needle to weave the tails down the centers of the tassels and into the tassels themselves. Make necessary adjustments to the length of the tassels. Join in the seam that runs down the waistband of one of the colors, A. To make a belt loop, chain 1.5 rows tightly "/4 centimeter, tie a knot at the end, and sew it to the side seam. It should be repeated on the other hem.

BABY CROCHET SHOES

The process of crocheting baby shoes is fun and efficient, and the finished product is adorable. They are beneficial in various contexts, including but not limited to extending congratulations to a new mother or making a charitable contribution to a hospital. Still, their applications are not restricted to these. It won't be long before the temptation to make more and more of these adorably cute baby shoes become an addiction for you.

Materials:

These shoes, made from Drops Cotton Merino, are very gentle and may be worn close to a baby's sensitive skin without causing any irritation. Because of their shape and the material's robustness, these shoes will make little feet feel safe, and the straps will protect them from slipping out of position.

You may discover a free pattern for a baby 0–3 months old right here on this page if that is what you are searching for. If you would like to construct them in a different size, the pattern for the Crochet.

Drops Cotton Merino, 50 grams

Crochet needle size: 3.50 mm

Scissors

Needles for darning

Two 15 mm buttons are included.

Gauge

10 ST = 5 cm.

Abbreviation for "Stitch," sometimes written as "ST."

Chains (CH) (CH)

Slip Stitch, abbreviated as SL ST

"Single crochet" is what "SC" stands for.

Half Double Crochet is abbreviated as HDC.

The abbreviation for "half double crochet increase" is "HDC INC" (Half double crochet 2 in the same ST.)

"Half double crochet decrease" is what "HDC DEC" stands for in crochet lingo (Half double crochet two together)

The initials DC stand for a double crochet stitch.

The abbreviation for double crochet decrease is "DC DEC" (Double crochet two together)

Observe and Make Notations on a Pattern

Size: 0-3

There are 9 millimeters between the heel and the ball of a person's foot.

The difficulty level is considered to be moderate.

The design makes extensive use of American crochet terminology throughout.

Instructions for the size 0-3 months

The Deepest Part

CH 10

In the first CH following the hook, HDC INC was awarded the HDC INC. round 1. HDC in each of the subsequent seven CCs. In the very last CC, HDC number 6. (You'll be working on the other side of your Chains from this point on.) H.D.C. inserted into CH7. Consider that the HDC INC of this ST is identical to that of the CH you started with. First ST SL (24 HDC). CH 1.

In the second round, the (34 HDC) SL ST was placed in the first ST, the HDC INC was established in the second ST, the HDC was placed in the third ST, the HDC INC was rated in the fourth ST, the HDC was placed in the fifth ST, and the HDC was established in the final ST.

The third round will begin with "HDC INC in the first ST. HDC in the following ST." Repeat the steps starting with *-* one more time. The following 7 STs will be HDC, then the next ST will be *HDC INC, and then the following ST will be HDC. There should be six iterations of the symbol *-*. Look for the letters HDC, HDC Inc., or HDC at the following seven stops. Repeat the steps beginning with * and ending with * for the second time. (44 HDC). In the first ST, slip the first stitch. Ch 1

Procedure:

The Most Important Part

The HDC requirement applies to all the fourth and final round starting places. Only do your actions inside the feedback loops. (44 HDC). Let's begin with the slip stitch in chain one.

The HDC will continue for the next 16 ST rounds. It is needed to perform the following instruction six times: *HDC DEC in the following ST. HDC in the following ST. * HDC in the last ten steps (38 ST) and SL ST at the beginning of the process. CH 1.

In the following fifteen STs, there will be six instances of HDC, followed by six instances of DC DEC. The first 11 ST. (CH 1) are SL ST., while the latter 11 ST. (32 ST) are HDC.

Following the seventh cycle, every ST will transition into an SC. Remember to finish off the yarn by tying it off and cutting it.

A Strap to Go with It

Attach the yarn to the top edge of the shoe. Approximately at the exact middle of it all.

Work a double crochet in the third chain from the hook as well as the next nine chains (10 DC)

To secure the strap, you will need to make an SL ST in the outside sole of the shoe.

Put your button in the slot on the lateral side of the shoe.

You may now secure the strap by making a buttonhole in one of the gaps between your DC ST and inserting it through the belt.

Make another set of shoes that are an exact duplicate of the first for the other foot, but this time connect the strap to the other side of the second pair of shoes. This will guarantee that you have a shoe for each foot in your collection.

Do you want to know how it feels to crochet with raffia, whether or not it will do damage to your hands, and whether or not it can be manipulated to your whims? Then continue reading to learn more about my experiences working with this fun paper media while I was crocheting.

When I have the chance to crochet with new material, it never fails to astonish me how yarn and thread can be transformed into art in the shape of fabric and decorations for the house using the skills of fiber artists like us. I couldn't help but feel like the princess in Rumpelstiltskin as I crocheted with golden white raffia that crumpled and rustled. More accurately, I felt like I was changing paper into a stylish and subtle market bag.

Working with various materials and seeing how simple stitches are transformed into complex patterns in each one is a satisfying experience for me. The look of a single crochet stitch with raffia will be different from the face of a single crochet stitch that worked, for example, with mohair. In addition, if the ingredients used to make your yarns are varied, you have an additional justification for keeping a more significant stockpile than is necessary.

Do you find that working with raffia causes your hands to get sore?

This is the first question that comes to me whenever I consider raffia. Given that it seems and feels like straw, is it possible to draw a parallel between working with it and baling hay? … In contrast to what I was anticipating, the raffia in question is not very rough.

When I was working with the butcher's twine, my hands suffered a lot more than they are now, but not quite as much. Raffia may be challenging, but because of its low weight, it is not difficult to manipulate in any way.

Because the Paper Gangster Bag is built from the bottom up, I found that as it became more significant, the inside of my arm felt more irritated by it. When the constant rubbing got too much for me to handle while crocheting, I would cover the bag with a tea towel so I would not get distracted.

Does raffia withstand bending and twisting while it's being used in crocheting?

Knitting and crochet are two forms of needlework that entail creating loops using a substance known as "yarn." Because it is formed of paper, raffia may give the impression that it is less malleable than other materials due to its composition. Although raffia is not as flexible as other materials, it may still be easily molded into the desired form. The paper has a unique, "rough" look due to the sharp angles and curves that are cut into it. Since the gauge loops cannot be easily altered, you must be very careful about the sizes you produce. However, I've discovered that the texture of the raffia can hide any little gauge difficulties, so everything turns out okay in the end!

Could you please tell me whether raffia is a lightweight material?

It's hard to think that this raffia has such a fluffy texture. As soon as I removed the skeins from their packaging, the first thing that struck me was how feathery and airy they seemed.

It only took me a little over one and a half skeins of Ra-Ra Raffia to finish the bag, but it scarcely seems like I'm carrying it about.

The following summarizes how many yards you may anticipate from a ball made of different materials weighing 100 grams.

Ra-Ra Raffia, made entirely of wood, has 273 yards or 250 meters for every 100 grams.

One hundred fifty-five yards (142 meters) of lustrous joyful cotton for every 100 grams (100 percent Pima cotton).

Be Safe This mohair mix consists of 78% kid mohair, 13% wool, and 9% polyamide, and it can be spun into 200 meters of yarn from only one hundred grams.

How does it feel about going around with the crocheted bag on your shoulder?

The outside of my reusable shopping bag has a feel that is a little bit rough. Although it is more challenging to work with than a gorgeous straw hat, it won't do as much damage to your hands as dealing with a sisal mat would. I haven't had any problems with it getting caught on anything up to this point, but I wouldn't want to wear anything delicate, like a sweater, while carrying it about with me.

Is it feasible to determine if the raffia yarn and the market bag that it produces will last for a long time?

I was unsuccessful in my effort to tie two hanks of yarn together by utilizing my tried-and-true method of invisible knotting, which requires some pulling to tighten. As a result, the raffia became broken.

The friction caused by the paper secured the square knot I used to link the skeins together after I tied them together. While working with raffia, I could not identify any points of vulnerability in its structure. A significant amount of pulling power was necessary to break in the way it did.

Because it is constructed out of a network of loops and knots, the bag has excellent elasticity and is long-lasting. I went to the local farmer's market and purchased over 20 navel oranges in addition to a variety of lemons and limes, all of which I am excited to try. Even though the bag swelled in size as it sagged, it could still contain everything without any problems.

Techniques for Raffia Crochet

Roll it into a ball to start, but make sure it's not too compact before continuing. This manner of operation is noticeably more convenient than any of the others.

It's possible to tear raffia if you tug on it too quickly or with too much effort. It has been helpful for me to not pull too hard on the raffia if, every so often, I let go of the strain and let it recover itself on its own.

According to my experience, it has a sticky texture, most noticeable after washing one's hands or applying moisturizer. You must wait until your hands are dry before touching them. Raffia is a very sticky yarn, which makes it more prone to this issue than other types of yarn. However, almost any thread may be torn if you tug on it too firmly.

It is easier to pull a stitch tighter after working it if I work it loosely at first.

The sum in question is inconsequential.

Spend a little more time on it than you would, but try not to spend too much, especially in the beginning.

Conduct drills with the use of a gauge swatch. To develop a sense of it, all you need to do is put in the necessary time and effort. Create a swatch before moving on to the actual knitting of the hat.

If you need to frog the raffia, which removes the strands, untangle it very gently. Pulling on other loops and pieces of the thread will occasionally liberate a stitch that is difficult to extract, which I've discovered to be the case when the stitch is incredibly tenacious. It is not enough to pull more forcefully. It may break.

Raffia yarn will take on the appearance of being more compressed once it has been frogged. You should have no hope that it will recover from this. However, if you give it another round of crocheting, you should be able to have it looking as good as new. My findings suggest that the quality is only excellent for a limited number of frogging's before it deteriorates quickly. After this point, the quality is unacceptable.

Even though this may give the impression that working with raffia is a laborious material (ha-ha), it is rather pleasurable to deal with. After being crocheted, it becomes much more potent.

Raffia Hat

This raffia hat is made from sustainable materials, so it will only improve with age.

For a more traditional experience, try plaiting some raffia into your raffia hat, which either sex may wear. You won't need more than some straw and a needle to craft this hat yourself.

Materials:

Raffia (about five bunches) (around five gangs)

A needle with a very prominent pair of eyes

Embellishments may be put on as one sees fit (a feather, ribbon, or any other oddities)

Plait

Put on some music and gather a handful of raffia; ideally, you should buy one with 12 to 15 feet of strands.

You'll need three lengths of raffia for each third once you've tied it into a knot and cut it into thirds. You may want to use a book to hold up the tail to prevent the plait from unraveling. You have the option of plaiting either three or five strands together. As the number of raffia decreases, continue to weave in additional strands. To get started, double a length that is about seven meters long.

Swirl

Start in the middle and work your way outward to create a spiral around the knot, like a snail's shell. Perform a total of five rotations starting at the top of the head.

Sew

Start putting your raffia snail together by inserting the needle into an extended length of raffia and sewing it together. Untie the knot at the snail's beginning, and then secure the plait by wrapping the raffia around the end of the braid. To create a U shape with the plat, fold it in half to be centered. Sew the two ends together for a distance of around 5 centimeters. The snail will guide you in a circular motion throughout the process. After you have finished the first five rounds of stitching, you should try the hat on to see whether or not you need to add an extra game or two of stitching. If there is a good fit, begin bending your raffia downward in a vertical direction for about five revolutions. If there is not a good fit, continue to the next step.

Brim

Put it back on your head and make sure it fits properly. You may build the hat's brim horizontally if it works well, bending the plate.

Your beginning point should be five rounds, and you may assess how you feel afterward. You have total control over the breadth of the brim of the hat.

When you reach the back of the hat, you may finish the plait correctly by stitching it under the braid directly above it.

Trim

Eliminate any superfluous raffia.

Including the Border or Rim

Procedure:

Turn the braid so that it is facing away from the crown at a straight angle and then start stitching after the hat block is flush on the cork board. You'll want to slide the braid around the height as you sew gently. It is important not to pull too hard otherwise, the shape of the brim will be messed up.

The curve of your brim will be created when you sew the braid with your right hand while holding the braid at an angle with your left hand. It is possible to make specific alterations to the shape by the use of steam at a later period.

When the brim is nearly the perfect size, wrap the braid around so that it aligns with the center back of the hat, then measure another 8 inches (this will be the loose raffia you weave into the brim), and snip off the extra braid. Take the raffia out of the braid, and position it so that it is directly in the center of the front of the hat. While you are working to rebrand the raffia, cut off individual strands of raffia and taper the braid down to a width of 1/4 inch.

In the end, you should have around 8 inches of raffia that is not braided. Keep stitching in the same fashion until you are about 3/4 of an inch from the middle of the back, and then gently overlap the braid for roughly 2 inches. To complete the wrapping, use the curved needle to weave the loose ends of the raffia through the brim one at a time.

You may mold your hat using steam, but you should exercise caution. The heat from the steam can rapidly burn your skin, so be sure to use gloves resistant to high temperatures. Wrapping a dish towel over the inside of your hat and holding it over a kettle that is being heated can allow you to reshape the brim of your hat.

If you so choose, you may add a headband made of stretch terry. Make the headband 1 inch longer than the length it may be worn around your head comfortably while providing enough security. First, take one of the cut edges and fold it over half an inch, then pin it so that it overlaps the other half an inch, and then sew it. Pin a headband to the hat's crown, so it sits along the rim on the side of the hat that is not beside the brim.

Raffia Bag

Viscose, which consists exclusively of wood fiber, is used to manufacture raffia. It does not degrade quickly, is not harmful to the surrounding ecosystem, does not take in any moisture, and is simple to mold. Therefore, I'll show you how to transform it into a convenient handbag.

In addition, I think using this material might unlock a whole new universe of creative possibilities for crocheting.

Because it does not trap heat and has a high degree of breathability, I want to utilize it to make a summer hat and perhaps some other things that are themed around summer.

Following this website will always be up to speed on the most recent and cutting-edge designs. If you haven't already, join my email list right now so that you don't miss out on any of these free designs! Now, let's go on to the most exciting section.

Materials:

I have high hopes that you will find this crochet purse tutorial to be helpful. It is easy to use and does not need any extra features or bells and whistles that are not essential. Enjoy!

If you found this one helpful, you may also be interested in the bag designs below.

Three crochet bags: two shoulder bags and one clutch. All are crochet.

It was necessary to use the majority of one skein of raffia yarn in tiling.

crochet hook with a diameter of 4 millimeters

Scissors

Needle for yarn

Identifier of the stitch

*By using the affiliate links included within these materials, I can make a small percentage of any sales. You are helping keep the lights on while saving money, time, and energy.

The Kind of Stitch and the Number of Threads That Were Used (US Term)

Stich is short for chain stitch.

"stich" is an abbreviation for the word "stitch" (es)

Single crochet is always worked in the same manner.

A single crochet spike stitch is denoted by the abbreviation "scalp." To do this, you need to knit a single crochet stitch in the row below the one you are now working on.

The acronym REP represents the word "repeat" in this particular instance.

YO is an acronym for "yarn over hook."

to millimeters

Confidence levels are low.

It should equal around 4 inches combined with 15 stitches and 19 rows.

Measurements come in at a width of 7.6 inches and 8.42 inches.

Procedure:

The stitch marker must always be worked into the first stitch of each new round when using the spiral knitting technique. This serves as a helpful reminder.

During the first round, you will chain 29 and perform a single crochet stitch into the second chain from the hook and each chain across. Afterward, during the second round, you will complete a single crochet stitch into each chain along the opposite side. There are a total of 56 stitches in this.

Repeat around, working two single crochet stitches into the first stitch, one single crochet stitch into the next stitch, and one single crochet stitch into each stitch after that while following the pattern established by the *. a total of 57 stitches

To complete the third round, start single crochet into the next stitch. A total of 57 stitches

In the fourth round, you will work as follows: *1 single crochet, one step into the next set* REP from *too* around until there is only one stitch left, and then single crochet into the last stitch. A total of 57 stitches (Check the picture below)

The construction of a crocheted bag using a spike stitch, with accompanying illustrations

Repeat from *too* around until only one stitch is left, then sc2tog in the remaining stitch. Repeat from *TO* around. This brings an end to Round 5. The total is 57 stitches (Check the picture below)

A crochet pattern for a clutch, with instructions and photographs of the finished item.

Fifteen more repetitions of Rounds 4 and 5 have to be completed. There will be 35 total rounds.

Rep Set 3 (Rounds 36 - 40)

At the end of round 40, cut the yarn and weave it in the ends to complete the project.

Handbag Strap, Crocheted

I crocheted the strap for my purse using an I-cord as my material.

You will chain three stitches for the first row and then leave a tail of around 6 inches. Put the hook through the second chain stitch from the hook, then YO to bring up a loop. You may create a loop by placing the theme into the next chain stitch and drawing it up through the YO.

You will hook onto the next stitch in the chain and use the YO to pull up a loop. There are three strands on the hook (Check the picture below)

The steps involved in making an I-cord strap are as follows:

At the beginning of the second row, you will need to remove two loops from your crochet hook (Make sure not to lose them). Please create a new circle by making a yarn over it and drawing it through the remaining loop on the hook. Next, a theme is introduced into the next loop, and a YO is used to draw up a circle. A pin is put into the next loop, and a loop is pulled up using a YO. The clip is made up of a total of three strands (Check the picture below)

The Crochet Strap: Directions for Next Steps

The strap length should be between 40 and 42 inches, but it may be adjusted to fit any measurement by simply repeating row 2.

To complete the I-Cord, you will meet one chain stitch with three loops on the hook before moving on to the next row. When you cut the yarn, you shouldn't forget to leave a tail that is six inches long.

MAKE SURE THAT THE STRAPS ARE ATTACHED TO THE CHANEL BAG.

We will use the tails we left on the straps and sew them into the purse on both sides. This will be done using the yarn needle. I usually start stitching around three rows down from the highest point on the bag; however, this may be changed to fit your tastes if you want.

TEDDY BEAR

This free crochet teddy bear design by Lucy Pollock is a win-win situation for everyone involved since no kid can have excessive teddies, and adults never get tired of making them. Our crochet teddy bear has a modern spirit while looking to be a traditional ted owing to his stripy pom-pom cap, adorable scarf, and denim dungarees. This is because our teddy bear was made using current crochet techniques. You may make him by working in the round with double crochet and doing some simple increases and reductions as you go. This adorable crochet bear just takes four distinct colors of the reasonably priced DK yarn that Style craft offers. For those just starting this enjoyable activity, our article entitled "How to Crochet Amigurumi" provides some valuable ideas you may use.

If you are interested in creating even cuter toys for children, we also have a free crochet pattern for a Medusa doll and a free pattern for a pom bear. These are also available for download. There is also a tutorial available for you to follow if you would instead learn how to crochet baby booties.

Materials:

What you'll want

Each of the following colors will need one ball of Style craft Special DK (or another brand of DK yarn):

Stone

Denim

Plum

Black

Crocheting needle size 4mm

The needle that is used in embroidery

Identifier of the stitch

Filling for toys

Pins (optional)

"Safety eyes" have a length of two inches and are black.

a pair of 9mm buttons, brown and black

Measurements

Approx. 31 centimeters is the average height of a human person (12in).

Tension

Although tension isn't significant for this project, you should check that your stitches are sufficiently close enough to prevent the stuffing from showing through.

Before donning dungarees, one should finish working on one's physique. After the bear's first and second legs have been built and connected, the head and body of the bear are made concurrently as a single continuous piece of fabric. It is much less difficult to adjust the straps and buttons of the dungarees after the teddy has been placed on them.

The whole list of the notations we use is included in the abbreviations and conversions reference. The directions for crocheting this teddy bear are written in British English; however, with the guidance provided, they are easily translated into American English.

Procedure:

First Things First

Stone can help you crochet a magic loop for your project.

The initial round of the magic loop is worked in double crochet and consists of eight stitches. Eight stitches

Work two double crochets into each stitch on the second round of the project. There are a total of sixteen stitches.

Continue with seven more repetitions of the third round's stitch pattern (DC, 2 DC in the next stitch). That is a significant number of stitches [there are 24 of them]

Work 4–6 double crochet stitches into each stitch around the circumference. (There are 24 stitches)

In the seventh round, make seven double crochets, work a dc2tog five times, and finish with seven double crochets. [19 stitches] should be counted.

Row 8: 5 double crochet, dc2tog 4 times, six double crochets. To a total of fifteen stitches according to the count

For rounds 9-16, do a double crochet in each stitch. (Number of Stitches: 15)

Prepare to fire! (First leg only).

The journey has now reached its second and last stage.

Proceed normally, but don't knot off the rope's end as you did in the previous leg. The back of the leg to the front of the leg requires about four double crochets.

On the 17th round, chain three stitches. Join dc stitches to the first leg as your starting point (line both legs together to get the correct stitch). Work dc stitches around the edge, going through both sides of the three chain stitches. This will finish the border. (Forty-one Needle Punctures)

It's possible to pack the legs.

For rounds 18-21, work a double crochet in each stitch around. This has a total of 36 stitches in its construction.

Round 22 will be performed four times (8 double crochets, two double crochets in the following stitch). A total of forty stitches

Make 23 double crochets in the next stitch after you've inserted the hook into the first stitch of the following [40 stitches] row.

Four times over, repeat Round 24. (9dc, 2dc in next stitch). "(44 stitches)"

To finish the circle, work 25 double crochet stitches into each of the following [44 stitches].

There must be a total of four repetitions of Round 26. (10dc, 2dc in next stitch). (forty-eight stitches)

The instructions for the design need 27 double crochets to be worked into each of the 48 stitches around the ring.

Repeat Round 28 (11 double crochets, then two double crochets in the next stitch) four more times. (Stitches = 52)

Work 29 double crochet stitches into the first thread around the whole circumference. (Stitches: 52)

In Round 30, it happened four times (12 double crochets, two double crochets in the following stitch). By use of [56 stitches]

This bouclé bear crochet pattern was designed by Kalaburagi and will appeal to you if you are looking for more crochet teddy bear patterns to add to your collection. This adorable teddy bear is made with loopy bouclé yarn and has a style that is quite typical for teddy bears. The pattern also includes instructions for making a wonderful bunny friend go along with the bear. On Etsy, you may be able to find the way.

Instructions for crocheting plush animals may be obtained on the website Kalaburagi.

Work a double crochet in each stitch around rounds 31 – 33. by use of [56 stitches]

Four times more, perform Round 34. (12 dc, dc2tog). (Number of Stitches: 52)

Work 35 rounds of double crochet into each stitch all the way around. (Stitches: 52)

Iterate Round 36 four times (11dc, dc2tog). (forty-eight stitches)

Work 37 double crochets into the middle of each stitch to complete the circle. (forty-eight stitches)

Iterate Round 38 four times (10dc, dc2tog). "(44 stitches)"

Work 39 double crochets into each stitch all the way around. "(44 stitches)"

Continue with Round 40 (4 times: 9 double crochets, dc2tog). A total of forty stitches

Put 41 double-crochet stitches into the first stitch of each round. A total of forty stitches

Four times over, repeat Round 42. (4 sets of 8dc, dc2tog). This has a total of 36 stitches in its construction.

Start a new round of double crochet in the next stitch around. Make 43 of them. This has a total of 36 stitches in its construction.

Things to take note of at this location.

Round 44 will be repeated six times (4dc, dc2tog). To fix this, we will need [30 stitches].

Work 45 double crochets into each stitch as you move around the circle. This sentence will be embroidered a total of thirty times.

Do Round 46 (six double crochets, double crochets together) five more times. (There are 24 stitches)

Work 47 double crochets into each stitch's middle stitch, so the circle is complete. (There are 24 stitches)

Six complete rotations of Round 48 (2dc, dc2tog). (Number of Stitches: 18)

Work 49 double-crochet stitches into each stitch around the circumference. [18sts]

Perform fifty stitches of work (6 rounds of 1dc, dc2tog). [12 stitches] are counted as one.

Create a double crochet stitch in each stitch around, for a total of 51 double crochet stitches. A total of twelve stitches

Put anything in this space, and then go on with the process.

This round consists of 12 repetitions of the 2dc stitch. (There are 24 stitches)

Six times more, repeat Row 53. (3dc, 2dc in next stitch). This sentence will be embroidered a total of thirty times.

A repeat of Round 54 (for a total of six times) (4 dc, two dc in next stitch). This has a total of 36 stitches in its construction.

Six times more, repeat Round 55. (5 dc, two dc in next stitch). [42 stitches] all in total

Repeat Round 56 six times, resulting in 48 stitches (6dc, 2dc in the next stitch).

It will take you six times to complete Round 57, which consists of seven double crochets followed by two double crochets in the next stitch. In all, there were [54 stitches]

Six times more, repeat Round 58. (8 double crochet, two double crochets in next stitch). [Sixty stitches] are going to be there.

Work one double crochet into each stitch around rounds 59–66. *Sew on the eyes between rounds 61 and 62, leaving a gap of 12 stitches between each eye, for a total of [60 stitches].

Continue with five more repetitions of Round 67 (dc8, dc2tog). Count of Stitches: 54

It would be best if you repeated Round 68 six times using the following pattern: (7dc, dc2tog). (forty-eight stitches)

Six times more, perform Round 69. (6 double crochets, dc2tog). [42 stitches] all in total

Complete six rounds of 70 repetitions (5dc, dc2tog). This has a total of 36 stitches in its construction.

Round 71 will be repeated six times (4dc, dc2tog). This sentence will be embroidered a total of thirty times.

Six times more, repeat Row 72. (3dc, dc2tog). (There are 24 stitches)

Things to take note of at this location.

Chain 73, then work a double crochet two together, followed by another double crochet two together. Repeat this pattern six times. (Number of Stitches: 18)

Six times more, repeat round 74, working one double crochet and dc2tog. A total of twelve stitches

Repeat the Dc2tog pattern 75 times with that number of stitches. Count of stitches: 6

A seam and a knot should be used to close the hole.

If you are interested in creating more adorable stuffed creatures, you may want to look at these additional free crochet amigurumi designs.

There is a free crochet pattern available of a whale.

Free instructions for crocheting an amigurumi cat are currently available.

A pattern for crocheting an amigurumi rabbit that you are free to use in any way you see fit.

The most delicate 40 amigurumi designs

Free pattern for crocheting a whale.

Mouth

Stone can help you crochet a magic loop for your project.

Work six rounds of double crochet into the first round. Count of stitches: 6

Work two double crochets into each stitch on the second round of the project. A total of twelve stitches

Six times more, repeat Row 3: (1dc, 2dc in next stitch). (Number of Stitches: 18)

It is necessary to repeat the fourth and fifth stitches of the previous round twice. (There are 24 stitches)

Repeat Round 5 (for a total of six times) (3 dc, two dc in the next stitch). This sentence will be embroidered a total of thirty times.

Do a double crochet stitch for 6–9 rounds in each stitch. This sentence will be embroidered a total of thirty times.

Ss, then fasten off, being sure to leave a long tail that may be used for stitching later on.

Arms (make 2)

Stone can help you crochet a magic loop for your project.

Work six rounds of double crochet into the first round. Count of stitches: 6

Work two double crochets into each stitch on the second round of the project. A total of twelve stitches

Six times more, continue with Round 3. (3 dc, two dc in next stitch). (Number of Stitches: 15)

Work 4–6 double crochet stitches into each stitch around the circumference. (Number of Stitches: 15)

Iterate Row 7 five more times (1dc, dc2tog). (Ten stitches)

For rounds 8–29, double crochet in each stitch around. 1 row of stitches

Ss, then tie off, leaving a tail that is enough length to weave in the ends of the work. When stuffing, you should never use anything other than your hands.

This pattern for dungarees to be crocheted for a teddy bear is provided free of charge.

Dungarees (first leg)

When sewing denim, start at the hem of one of the legs.

You will start the first round by chaining 18 stitches and working a slip stitch into the first chain you made. This will create a circle for you to work in. (Number of Stitches: 18)

Work other double crochet round into each stitch between rounds 2 and 8. Ss on only the first leg (there should be 18 stitches).

The journey has now reached its second and last stage.

At least up to Round 8, the process will be the same as in the last leg.

The ninth round begins with a chain of four and a slip stitch to the first stitch. Next, finish one full game of double crochet, working into the front and back of each chain stitch [44 stitches].

Work a double crochet stitch into the surrounding chain's tenth, thirteenth, and fourteenth stitches. "(44 stitches)"

Four times through Round 14's repetitions (10 dc, two dc in next stitch). (forty-eight stitches)

First, insert the hook into the next stitch and double-crochet it 15 times. (forty-eight stitches)

Repeat Round 16 (11 double crochets, then two double crochets in the next stitch) four more times. (Number of Stitches: 52)

17 double crochets worked into each of the 52 stitches around the circumference (one circle)

Four times through Round 18's repetitions (12 double crochets, two double crochets in the next stitch). by use of [56 stitches]

Work 19 rows of double crochet into every single stitch between rows 19 and 23. by use of [56 stitches]

Repeat Round 24 (eight groups of five double crochets, dc2tog) seven more times. (forty-eight stitches)

First, insert the hook into the next stitch and double-crochet it 25 times. (forty-eight stitches)

Repeat Round 26 a total of eight times (4dc, dc2tog). A total of forty stitches

Round 27, and you should double-crochet in each stitch. A total of forty stitches

Four times, do the instructions for Round 28 (work eight double crochets and double crochet together). This has a total of 36 stitches in its construction.

Work 29 double crochet stitches into the first thread around the whole circumference. This has a total of 36 stitches in its construction.

Perform a total of four rounds of 30. (7 double crochets, dc2tog). That is a significant number of stitches (there are 32 of them).

Work 31–33 double crochet stitches into the next stitch around. Count: [3 2]

Put your foot on the brake and go into ss. Put the thread's ends inside the needle.

In our family, it is essential to have groovy dungarees for teddy bears. If you like dressing up stuffed animals, you won't want to pass up the opportunity to make the super-adorable Dress-up bears amigurumi design that Ilaria Calibri created. It includes three beautiful outfits. On Etsy, you may be able to find the pattern.

Crochet designs for teddy bears designed by Airlie Design

Straps (make 2)

When working with denim, it's ideal to begin with, a long yarn that may be stitched in when the project has been completed. Ch25.

To begin the first round, work two double crochet stitches into the second chain from the hook. Dc stands for "crosswise," which refers to the direction of labor. The first turn of Chapter 1. (There are 24 stitches)

Work two double crochet stitches in the next available space across. (There are 24 stitches)

After finishing the stitch, leave a long tail for weaving in the loose ends. (The circumference of each strap will be 5 inches.)

Toggle clasps (make 2)

The dungarees' natural waist should be your size's starting point. There are four stitches to the right of the center. Ss the Denim yarn into the next stitch, chain three, and then ss into the same stitch to create the initial loop of the pattern. Cut a long piece of yarn and use it to cover the exposed ends.

In the left loop, you will make a repetition of the sixth stitch from the right circle.

Free pattern for a crochet teddy bear cap to work up.

Hat

Make a crochet magic loop using the denim yarn.

The first round consists of six double crochet stitches worked in the loop. Count of stitches: 6

Work two double crochets into each stitch on the second round of the project. A total of twelve stitches

Instead, use the color Plum in its stead.

Six times more, repeat Row 3: (1dc, 2dc in next stitch). (Number of Stitches: 18)

It is necessary to repeat the fourth and fifth stitches of the previous round twice. (There are 24 stitches)

Denim should be your new go-to fabric.

A repeat of Round 5 (for a total of six times) (3 dc, two dc in next stitch). This sentence will be embroidered a total of thirty times.

Six times go through the motions of Round 6 (four double crochets, then two double crochets in the next stitch). Change to the plum-colored yarn (36 stitches).

Seven iterations of the seventh round (5 dc, two dc in next stitch). [42 stitches] all in total

Six times more, do Round 8's actions (6 dc, two dc in next stitch). When you get to the 48th stitch, change to the denim color.

Perform Round 9 six times (7 dc, two dc in the next stitch). Count of Stitches: 54

It is essential to continue switching up the colors every two rounds.

10-21 double crochets in each stitch around. Count of Stitches: 54

Take the hook out of the yarn, then knot off the end, leaving a long tail for seaming (if you want to sew the hat to the head, go with a long piece of yarn).

Ears (make 2)

Stone can help you crochet a magic loop for your project.

Work six rounds of double crochet into the first round. Count of stitches: 6

Work two double crochets into each stitch on the second round of the project.

 A total of twelve stitches

Six times more, repeat Row 3: (1dc, 2dc in next stitch). (Number of Stitches: 18)

For rounds 4-8, do a double crochet in each stitch. (Number of Stitches: 18)

Ss, and then tie off, being sure to leave a long tail to sew the hat's brim.

Pom-pom

Plum will assist you with wrapping the yarn around your three fingers twenty times. To get started, cut a considerable portion of the string. After removing the cord from your fingers, tightly wrap the remaining yarn around the object's center. Use the scissors to remove any unnecessary loops. Snip off the extra thread to make the pom-pom seem more spherical, but be sure to leave a long tail so you can sew it onto the cap afterward.

Scarf

To get started on your Plum project, begin by working with a long strand of yarn that you can use to weave in the ends of the stitches.

Ch 61.

Work a double crochet stitch in the second chain from the hook and across the rest of the chains using a double crochet hook. The first turn of Chapter 1. [Sixty stitches] will be there.

Repeat the dc sequence in the next stitch, chain 1, and turn around. [Sixty stitches] are going to be there.

After this round, Row 2 is worked again without rotating the work.

Before you secure the yarn, be sure to leave a long tail for weaving in the ends.

The previous page features the free crochet pattern for a teddy bear.

make amends

Before you finish stitching it on the lips, ensure that the head is evenly stuffed with the stuffing (use your pins to help keep it in place while sewing). It would help if you positioned your nose so that it is in the middle of the mouthpiece and then used some black yarn to sew it there, being careful to go back and forth in the duplicate threads. To indicate the mouth, draw a line pointing downward. Create two eyebrows using the same yarn by laying them on top of the eyes in the appropriate positions. Before you put on the hat, check to see that the black string is firmly attached to the back of your head. This is necessary if you want the yarn to remain concealed.

You should attach the ears to the hat. Before you sew the cap on Teddy, you should connect the pom-pom to the top of the lid to complete the appearance. Bind any threads that are hanging free.

Fix the holes in the pants. To the right shoulder strap, attach the buttons. Put the button in the buttonhole, pull the belt over the front of your neck and crisscross it to the other side of your back. Repeat the process with the second strap, then sew the back straps to the dungarees for an added protection layer. Because this is the only method to establish where the straps should be attached, the bear must be dressed in the dungarees for this to work correctly.

Use stitches to mend the edges of the scarf that have frayed. If you do not want the scarf to fall off the teddy bear, you can either knot it around the bear's neck or sew it into place.

BAT

If you are looking for a Halloween crochet project that is easy to do but also impressive, the free bat crochet pattern Sara Huntington designed is an excellent option. This amigurumi bat has loops for feet, enabling it to firmly attach itself to whatever surface you choose.

We have some resources that will benefit you if you are new to the craft of amigurumi and want to construct this free crochet pattern of a bat.

Materials:

What you'll want

You are free to use whatever dark-colored DK yarn you choose (maybe some black Hayfield Bonus DK acrylic yarn in the 100g/280m range), but keep in mind that the gauge will be different.

Size of the hook: 2.5 millimeters (US size B/1 or C/2)

Eye protection devices

The stuffing for toys

Needles for tapestry

Identifier of the stitch

A quantity of a modest, dark-colored felt

Measurements

Measuring in at just 13 cm or 5 inches in height

The whole list of the notations we use is included in the abbreviations and conversions reference.

Procedure:

This amigurumi crochet design for a bat is an accessible and enjoyable activity for those who are just starting. Continue working in a spiral pattern that never ends, but don't stop to do a slip stitch at the end of each round. To keep track of how far you've come, place a stitch marker in the very first stitch of each game and work your way up from there.

Head

Make a "magic loop" in crochet using black yarn and the technique.

In the first round (RS), make chain 1 (which does not count as a stitch) and then work eight double crochet stitches into the loop. A total of eight stitches

The second round is worked by inserting two double crochet stitches into each double crochet around. There are a total of sixteen stitches.

Continue with Round 3 eight more times (1 dc in the next dc, two dc in the next dc). (There are 24 stitches)

Work a double crochet into each of the existing double crochets for rows 4-11.

Round 12 was completed eight times (Dc in the next stitch, dc2tog). There are a total of sixteen stitches.

Work 13 double crochets into the stitches that are considered the start and end of the round.

Four times through Round 14's repetitions (Dc in next two sets, dc2tog). A total of twelve stitches

Make 15 double crochets in the middle of the following double crochet.

Body

It is advised to go through Round 16 at least four times in practice (Dc in the next two stitches, 2dc in the next stitch). There are a total of sixteen stitches.

Work one double crochet into each double crochet surrounding you as directed in the pattern for rounds 17-22.

Avoid securing anything at all costs. Adjust the number of stitches that separate the eyes so that there are six of them between Rounds 10 and 11. Stuff the head as well as the body firmly. During the last round of the Body flat exercise, you want to ensure that your eyes are focused in the middle of your face. Finish by working eight single crochet stitches across the body's base, being sure to slide your hook through both the front and back of each stitch. Complete the task and tuck away the loose ends.

The first action

Black should be used for the initial stitch, and the seam should be joined with ss.

The first row is worked in a single crochet pattern, which consists of the following steps: chain one (this does not count as a stitch), double crochet in the same stitch and the next two stitches, turn and continue working in the remaining stitches. [3 dc]

Ch 1 (does not count as a stitch), dc in each dc across, turn. Rows 2-9: Repeat Row 2-9. Count of stitches: 3. Complete the knot using a long tail.

Insertion of the Other Foot in Sequence

You should skip the following two stitches when working on the ss seam. Repeat Rows 1-9, connecting Black in the next stitch of each successive row. When you are finished, be sure to leave a long tail. Fold each foot in half and use a tapestry needle and the long seat to connect the final row to the ss seam on the back of the bat. This will create a loop that may be used to hang the bat in an inverted position.

Ears (make 2) (make 2)

Construct a ring of mystic power with black.

First round (right side): work a single crochet to the top of the initial chain stitch-3, ch3 (counts as tr here and throughout), then 11 double crochets into the loop. A total of twelve stitches

When you are finished, be sure to leave a long tail. Attach the ears to the head using the image as a guide, and sew them into place after they are in the correct position.

Wings

Make cutouts of wings from the piece of black felt and use the image as a template. Make a pattern out of the photo, and glue or sew the pieces onto the head in the appropriate places.

HIPPO

This charming design features a little hippopotamus that is tiny enough to fit in the palm of your hand. He has a huge nose and short, stumpy legs, which is the topic of today's darling illustration.

This adorable tiny hippo may be crocheted at no charge using the free pattern.

Aside from some more intricate parts, such as the ears, legs, and tail, this is a straightforward project that can be completed in a couple of hours.

Size

When crocheted using DK weight cotton and a 2,50 mm hook, the finished product will be a little over three and a half inches (9,5 cm) in length, 5.5 cm (2 15") in height,

and measure a little over three and a half inches (9,5 cm) in width.

Materials:

Essential capacity to have

The ring that bestows power.

a method of knitting or crocheting worked in spirals

In a sequence

Worked in a single row of crochet stitches (double crochet stitch in the UK and Australia)

Increasing

Decreasing

Closing up loose ends

, putting the finishing touches on a task that has been finished.

Putting together something open in some places and closed in others with stitching.

Stitching a folded component together to make it into a closed piece.

Yarn. My choice of adventure was Novita "Tennessee," a DK-weight adventure made entirely of cotton. It has a length of 105 meters per 50 grams (115 yards per 50 grams), an 8-ply thread count, 11 stitches per inch, and a weight of 3: light. There will be a need for around 22 grams (50 meters) of yarn.

Use a crochet hook with a size ranging from 2.25 millimeters to 2.75 millimeters (US size 1/B to 2/C), or follow the instructions provided by the yarn manufacturer.

Stuffing materials include polyester fiberfill, wool, wadding, and other things.

Six millimeters (1/4 inch). You may use everything from buttons and beads to safety eyes and felt.

A spool of lovely pink cotton thread for embroidery is wound on a spool.

When working with yarn, you'll need a needle, scissors, and a stitch marker.

Procedure:

Insert the hook through the hole in the magic ring, then single crochet the desired number of times around the ring.

There is no difference between a chain stitch and a chain stitch.

The term "slip stitch" refers to the same thing as "slip stitch."

Making single crochet means "stitching in a single chain" (double crochet stitch in the UK and Australia).

This term indicates doing so to produce n single crochet stitches, with one stitch on each thread.

The increase is accomplished by working two single crochet stitches into the same space as the previous stitch.

Dec is short for "decrease," and it refers to the process of crocheting two stitches together to achieve an inconspicuous decrease.

(Single crochet, four increases) Multiplying by no means working the pattern inside the brackets n times.

When one entire round of knitting is done, there will be [36] stitches.

If the pattern doesn't specify otherwise, knit or crochet in a continuous spiral without connecting rounds or turning your work. If the design does set differently, turn your work.

Make sure you use a stitch marker or a spare piece of yarn to help you keep track of where you began and stopped each round, so you don't get confused. Following the conclusion of each round, the marker will move forward one space.

Every stitch should be done through both loops simultaneously unless the pattern specifically instructs you to do it differently.

Head

Mr., repeating the single crochet stitch six times in Round 1 equals [6].

This is the second round: [12] equals increase multiplied by 6.

Multiples of single crochet with an increment of 6 stitches for Round 3 equals [18].

(Increase, sc2) multiplied by six equals [24] for the fourth round.

Performing single crochet into the following four stitches (rounds 5-8) equals [24].

(sc2, dec) times five plus sc4 equals [19] for the ninth round.

A single crochet stitch in each of the stitches all the way around (Round 10) = [19]

In the eleventh round, you would work four single crochets, decrease, seven single crochet, four single crochet, and so on until you achieved the desired height.

The number [15] is what you get when you follow the pattern for Round 12: single crochet 5, decrease, single crochet 3, decrease, single crochet 5.

For rounds 13 and 14, [15] equals inserting a single crochet hook into each stitch around the project.

It is recommended that the safety eyes be placed between rows 12 and 13, on the side opposite the round end. There should be five stitches (4 holes) between the safety eyes.

You shouldn't be frightened to blow your nose repeatedly. Over the fifth round, the nostrils should be embroidered.

crochet animal patterns accessible at no cost

free hippopotamus amigurumi pattern

(Decrement in single crochet) multiplied by 5 in Round 15 = [10]

increase multiplied by five equals [5] for Round 16

You don't need to pack as much information into your mind anymore. When cutting the yarn, make sure to leave a long tail and then secure the end. Picking up the leftover stitches will allow you to close the hole.

a crochet design for a hippopotamus that does not cost anything at all

Ears (make 2) (make 2)

Mr., you will work five rounds of single crochet to equal [5].

For the second crochet round, make a single stitch into each existing stitch around = [5].

In the third round, you will single crochet, reduce by one, and skip the remaining stitches, equaling 4.

Simply inserting your needle into the next stitch will create a sly stitch. Cut the yarn, making sure to save a long tail for sewing, and set it aside. Never obstruct the ears of another person.

Finish knitting round 15 by stitching the ear flaps in a flat position.

How to Crochet a Hippopotamus Toy with These Step-by-Step Instructions

template for constructing amigurumi dolls

Body

Mr., repeating the single crochet stitch six times in Round 1 equals [6].

This is the second round: [12] equals increase multiplied by 6.

Multiples of single crochet with an increment of 6 stitches for Round 3 equals [18].

On the fourth round, [22] is calculated as follows: (single crochet 3, increase) x 4 + (single crochet 2)

Work a single crochet into each stitch of rounds 5-12 to finish the project = [22].

Repeat Round 12 until you have [18] ((single crochet 3, dec) x 4) + [2]).

Get everything you need to start packing the body.

The following pattern will be used during the fourteenth round: [12] = (single crochet, dec) x 6.

After multiplying dec by 6 to obtain the final score for Round 15, we got [6].

At long last, you are free to cease squeezing things into the body. When cutting the yarn, make sure to leave a long tail and then secure the end. Picking up the leftover stitches will allow you to close the hole.

The head will be attached to the body by making a few beautiful stitches below it.

Legs (make 4)

Mr., repeating the single crochet stitch six times in Round 1 equals [6].

Multiply the result of [9] by 3 in the second round (single crochet, increase).

[9] is the result of doing single crochet into the third and fourth rounds.

Simply inserting your needle into the next stitch will create a sly stitch. Cut the yarn, making sure to save a little tail for seaming. The legs must be filled very firmly.

Sewing should be used to attach the bottom body.

Get this free amigurumi pattern for a hippopotamus right now!

Tail

Tie a slip knot ten centimeters (about 4 inches) from the beginning of the yarn.

After you have finished making the fifth chain, you may cut the cord and fasten it off, leaving a tail about two inches in length. Insert the end of the excess yarn, around 10 centimeters or 4 inches, into the last chain. Pull the yarn tails inside and tighten the knot you have created so that they nearly touch the end of the yarn. Remove the extra thread by cutting it.

Attach a string to the rear of the tail.

The conclusion is as follows.

JELLYFISH

Jellyfish reach their maximum maturity at a length of 15–18 inches, and their heads have a diameter of around 5 inches. The size of your jellyfish will be determined by the number of curlicues you use and the pattern you arrange. After some strenuous play, the coiled tentacles of the jellyfish that belonged to my kid began to unwind and grow in length.

There is one item of advice or warning that I need to present you with. Please ensure you keep a watchful check on the younger children utilizing this. These long queues are twisted, and I pray to God that nobody dies due to being strangled by them. This is not a dangerous design, but accidents may happen when children are involved. Children should not be allowed to sleep with their jellyfish friends, and you should be cautious if you see them throwing it about. It's possible that keeping them confined to the bathroom as a cute towel would be the best option.

Our excellent reader, Jeannette Kemp, who translated this pattern into Dutch so that it might be shared with everyone, deserves a big thank you for her hard work.

Materials:

Clover Amour Hook*, size G (4.0 mm) hook

It would help if you noticed that even though I used a G hook for the top of the jellyfish, I tried out both a G hook and an H hook for the curly cues while making the blue and purple jellyfish.

Inspirations You will need two skeins of the primary color when working with Bernat Handcrafter Cotton Yarn, and you will only need one skein of the accent color.

The questionable jellyfish are either Robin's Egg or a Mod Blue. The colors of the purple kind of jellyfish range from violet to bright pink.

Eyewear with a Diameter of 9 millimeters for Protection

The black color of the DMC embroidery thread

Needles intended for use in embroidery

scissors

Utilization of Polyester for Use in Fiberfill

Terminology related to stitching: slip stitch

Stitching in chains, often known as chain stitching

crocheting with just one stitch at a time

a pair of stitches worked in half double crochet

The abbreviation "dc" in crochet refers to the "double crochet" stitch.

The abbreviation for the joining and decreasing stitch is "sc2tog" (single crochet two together).

How to Crochet a Jellyfish Detailed Instructions

Cap/Face

To begin, you will work eight single crochet stitches into the magic circle. This will complete the first round. Work a slip stitch into the top of the first single crochet to attach the pieces.

First, chain one, then work two single crochet stitches into the first and the subsequent stitches. This is how you start the second round. Work a slip stitch into the top of the first single crochet to connect.

Procedure:

Start with chain 1, work one single crochet into the next stitch, then two single crochets into the following stitch. Repeat the process many times. Join the second single crochet to the first one using a slip stitch.

The crocheting should look like this after the fourth round: chain one, then work one single crochet stitch into each of the next two stitches, followed by two single crochet stitches into the next. Repeat the process many times. Join the second single crochet to the first one using a slip stitch. (32)

5. Start with chain 1, and then work the following pattern around: *work one single crochet into each of the following three single crochet, then work two single crochets into the next single crochet* Repeat the process many times. Join the second single crochet to the first one using a slip stitch.

For the sixth round, you will chain 1, then work *1 single crochet into each of the following four stitches, two single crochets into the next stitch* Iterate again and again. Join the second single crochet to the first one using a slip stitch.

Round 7-8: Make a chain of 1, then single crochet into each stitch. Join the second single crochet to the first one using a slip stitch.

To begin the ninth round, chain 1, work one single crochet stitch into each of the next five stitches, followed by two single crochet stitches into the next stitch. Iterate this pattern as many times as desired. Join the second single crochet to the first one using a slip stitch. (56)

Beginning with the initial chain, work a single crochet stitch into each stitch around the circumference. Rounds 10 through 14 Join the second single crochet to the first using a slip stitch.

After starting with a chain one, you will single crochet into the following two stitches as instructed in the pattern for the fifteenth round. *Repeat the sequence of (sc2tog), single crochet in the next stitch, and sc2tog. Repeat the process many times. Join the second single crochet to the first one using a slip stitch.

Complete the task and tuck away the loose ends.

The lowermost part of a jellyfish.

In the first round, create a magic circle by chaining one and working eight single crochets into the process. Join the second single crochet to the first one using a slip stitch.

First, chain one, then work two single crochet stitches into the first and the subsequent stitches. This is how you start the second round. Join the single and double crochet to the first using a slip stitch.

Start with chain 1, work one single crochet into the next stitch, then two single crochets into the following stitch. Repeat the process many times. Join the second single crochet to the first one using a slip stitch.

The crocheting should look like this after the fourth round: chain one, then work one single crochet stitch into each of the next two stitches, followed by two single crochet stitches into the next. Repeat the process many times. Join the second single crochet to the first one using a slip stitch.

In the fifth round, the third chapter (does not count as stitch). * After completing two double crochets into the next stitch, go on to the next stitch and perform single, double crochet into it. Repeat the process many times. Join the second single crochet to the first one using a slip stitch.

After you have left a tail that is sufficient length to work single crochet around, fasten off—at least some amount of separation (a few meters).

Jellyfish streamers and tentacles may be seen here.

Using the streamer's freestyle was the easiest and most enjoyable way to make a move. The differences aren't significant, and I focused on the same core concepts. I suggest looking over my curly cue sampler to understand the many curl designs available. Utilizing a different size hook is required to create an entirely new look. The blue ones were crocheted using a turn of size G, while the purple ones were worked with an H-sized hook. There are eight tentacles on each jellyfish, and their length and width may vary widely from animal to animal.

You may build a chain of thirty, forty, fifty, sixty, or seventy.

In each gap created by the chain, do either two (or three) single crochet stitches OR two (or three) partial double crochet stitches.

Work into the second chain from the hook to start a single crochet stitch. This is the second chain from the hook. Start your first half double crochet at the third chain from the hook if that's where you wish to put your turn.

Now, picture this as a crocheted version of one of those "Choose Your Own Adventure" books. Finish off the chain, making sure to leave a tail, then continue with either single or half double crochet, working 2 or 3 stitches into each chain across before fastening off.

My experience has shown me that the best results may be achieved by keeping a single pattern for the shortest time necessary to produce the desired curl, then moving on to a new practice to make a different loop form. Alternating between different kinds of stitches too often is not recommended. You have the option of either correctly curling the curly cues or leaving them in an untidy state.

Assembly

First, position a pair of safety eyes between rows 12 and 13 of the hat, roughly eight stitches apart.

The second step is to stitch a mouth in the center of the face, about in the exact location of the eyes.

Third, to join the tentacles' two tails to the bottom panel, you need to thread them through the holes in the panel's stitching and then double-knot them. Because it will be hidden inside the filled skull, you have the option of either weaving in the ends or not doing so. Because I was unsure of the force the children would pull on the tentacles, I decided to weave in the loose ends.

crochet-jellyfish-tutorial

Step four involves aligning the seam stitch on the panel with the seam stitch on the cap. Method of the front-to-back loop: Catch the back loop of a cap stitch and a tail loop on the board by hooking them together. Utilize a chain stitch for this. Inserting the hook into the space between the cap stitch and the first-panel stitch is the first step in making a single crochet. After that, a loop has to be pulled through, and the single crochet stitch is complete. (If you have to, fudge this. After you have joined the two sides, it is in working order and ready to use.

Fifth, enter the hook through all four loops on the next stitch and each stitch around from the outside of the hat (cap and panel). Perform a single stitch of crochet.

Step six involves packing the head with fiberfill and continuing to work in single crochet around the outside of the skull until it is finished. When connecting to the initial single crochet, use a slip stitch to make the connection. Complete the task and tuck away the loose ends.

To make the jellyfish suitable for hanging, a loop may be sewn onto the top of the fish. If not, there will be no more play!

DINOSAUR

Because my next-door neighbor's child is obsessed with dinosaurs, I crocheted this ancient creature. She already had a significant number of dinosaur figurines and toys, but the one she desired the most was a baby one. Following some research,

I decided to undertake the challenge, and the end product is a dinosaur design for a Stegosaurus Rex.

Materials:

To complete my crochet dinosaur, I need some yarn and buttons.

The following are some more details.

Instructions on how to crochet a detailed dinosaur are supplied.

The Crochet Dinosaur Created by Cotton Nutty

CROCHET ACCESSORIES From the Prehistoric Era

YARN

Both Hobbit Baby Cotton Midi (for the body of the crochet dinosaur) and Hobbit Rainbow Cotton 8/8 yarn were used in the production of this item (for eggshells). This action was taken on my part for two different reasons. Since the toys were intended for a little girl, I first had to choose an age-appropriate yarn for children. Both threads are made entirely of natural fibers that have been given the OEKO-TEX certification, making them an excellent choice. Two, since I had never used it before, I was interested in learning how it felt and what it looked like. The Baby Cotton Midi is great and a breeze to work with, but overall, I am satisfied with both options.

The following is a list of the colors that I used and the quantity that I applied:

DINOSAUR Crochet in GREEN

Cotton to Comfort the Infant:

Green Eucalyptus, number 10, one skein

July, a few meters of clear sky blue, I will simply refer to as "blue."

It's a Rainbow, and it's Cotton, and it's a Size 8/9:

1.5 skeins of 053 pastel yellow (which I will just refer to as "yellow").

Dinosaur in PINK Crochet

Cotton to Comfort the Infant:

One solitary skein of pale rose color number 11 (which I shall refer to as "pink")

A few meters away, ten luxuriant Eucalyptus trees may be seen.

The Rainbow Cotton 8/8 for this week is as follows:

To complete this project, I will need 1.5 skeins of color #038, which I shall call violet.

SUBSTITUTES FOR YARN

Procedure:

You might substitute Babytalk Organic Cotton, Gazza Organic Baby Cotton, or Bernat Softie Baby Cotton for the Hobbit Yarn if you cannot locate it or want to purchase it online. You could also use Bernat Softie Baby Cotton if you cannot get it. These yarns are of the same quality in composition and weight, and they have all passed the required safety examinations. If you aren't worried about the certification status of the yarn, another option would be to try Lion brand 24/7 Cotton or HAC DIY Milk Cotton yarn.

FEATURED: CROCHET DINO PRODUCTS

To complete your Dino amigurumi craft, you will also need the following materials:

Hook, 3.5mm (US E-4)

Eye protection devices

The stuffing for toys

The use of pins to indicate sutures

The total amount of rows.

Needles for tapestry

Scissors

Have you considered adding some flavor to your plaything? Using some remarkable amigurumi decorations, you may set your plushie apart from the crowd.

TENSION/GAUGE

Work 18 stitches in single crochet and 20 rows for a square with a dimension of 10 centimeters or 4 inches.

MEASUREMENTS THAT COULD BE CONCLUDED (egg with crochet dinosaur inside)

a person who has a height of 21 cm (8.5 inches)

12 centimeters in width (5 inches)

The depth is about 5 inches (12 cm).

Spellbinding Ring, Mr.

A single stitch is performed in crochet.

Corporation, Double Work

The combined decay of minus two

C stands for the chain.

Split is the acronym for the slip stitch.

BLO stands for "back-loop-only."

Double crochet, or dc.

Half-double crochet (dc)

CROCHET TERMS: "Treble" = "treble"

Continue moving forward while you are working in rounds unless otherwise advised.

It will make the thing seem more put together if the connections are seamless.

After each row, a number is enclosed in brackets representing the total number of stitches worked in that row. The monitoring should be improved if the processes are followed to the letter.

Declaration of Law Concerning the Ownership of Copyright for Pattern

CROCHET PATTERN IN THE FORM OF A DINOSAUR

The first phase in the process of making our crochet monster is putting together the body and head of the dinosaur. The next stage is constructing hands and feet and then attaching them to the creature's main body.

We give it its final appearance by adding details such as spikes and facial characteristics. The amigurumi dinosaur is placed into the crocheted egg in the last step.

BODY & MIND

Make a dinosaur out of green yarn by crocheting it and another relic out of pink yarn by crocheting it.

Rounds worked in single crochet in the middle row

You will move up one position in the first row, then move up one space once more, for a total of six times

You will single crochet and increase six times in the second row

You will increase by creating two single crochets in the third row, and then you will repeat the increase five more times after that

In the fourth row, you will make three single crochets, then four increases, then four single crochets, then four increases, and finally, you will perform three repeats of the pattern as follows: * three single crochets, three additions *

Repeat from * to the end of the row, working five single crochets, two increases, one single crochet, two increases, eleven single crochets, three single crochets, four increases, and six single crochets (38)

You will knit eight single crochet, three additions, and 27 single crochets across the sixth row

Row 7: start with eight single crochet stitches, increase by two double crochet stitches, increase by four double crochet stitches, and increase by 27 single crochet stitches (43)

Work 11 single crochet, two dc increases, and 30 single crochets across the eighth row (45)

Forty-five stitches worked in single crochet over rows 9-16.

Row 17: 10 single crochets, *decrease, one single crochet * 4 times, ten single crochets, *decrease, two single crochet * 3 times, single crochet

The pattern for Row 18 looks like this: 8 single crochet stitches, *decrease, one single crochet* four times, nine single crochet stitches, *decrease, one single crochet* three times (31)

Row 19 has the following progression: six single crochet, one decrease, one repeat, eight single crochet, one decrease, and three single crochets.

Work 3 single crochets, *decrease, one single crochet* 4 times, six single crochets, *decrease, one single crochet * twice, and three single crochets. This completes Row 20.

At this stage, you should finish filling the skull, and then on row 10 or 11, you should symmetrically connect the eyes.

The pattern for Row 21 is as follows: 4 single crochets, four double crochets, six single crochets, and one single crochet (16)

Crochet 2 single crochet, Dec 4 single crochet, six single crochets in Row 22.

You may make an increase by working one single crochet into the first stitch of the following stitch and then repeating this process another six times down the row (Row 23).

In the twenty-fourth row, you will work four single crochet stitches, *increase, one single crochet* three times, single crochet 6, increase 1, and then work one single crochet stitch.

The last row, number 25, is comprised of the following: four single crochets, one increase, one single crochet, five repeats of this pattern, five single crochets, two additions, and two single crochets. (28)

In Row 26, I did 11 single crochets, an increase, 13 single crochets, another increase, and two single crochets

In the 27th row, you will knit 12 single crochet stitches, an increase, and 17 single crochet stitches

Crochet 12 double crochets in row 28, then increase by one double crochet, then crochet 18 double crochets in row 29.

In row 29, work an increase, 13 single crochets, then 18 single crochet (33)

In row 30, begin with a foundation chain of 14, work an increase, and then work 18 single crochets.

In row 31, begin with a foundation chain of 15, work an increase, and then work 18 single crochets.

Fifteen single crochet stitches, one double crochet stitch worked into the next stitch, an increase of one double crochet stitch, and 19 single crochet stitches worked throughout Row 32.

In the 33rd row, you will work the following pattern: * single crochet 5, increase * 6 times

To make the increase, work six single crochet stitches into the next stitch, and then increase the number of stitches by six more in row 34.

Row 35 begins with an increase stitch worked into the first 22 stitches, followed by an extra increase stitch worked into the next 22 stitches

You will work 47 single crochet stitches in the leftover space after the rise in the middle of Row 36, and then you will work two single crochet stitches in the

In the 37th row, you will knit 48 single crochet stitches, then an increment, and finally two single crochet stitches

Start with 48 single crochets, work an increase, and then work three single crochets into the next stitch

Row 39 consists of an increase, followed by 49 rows of single crochet

For Row 40: Ch 9, * 3 single crochet, dec * 3 times, * dec, 3 single crochet * 3 times, * dec, 3 single crochet * 3 times, * dec, 3 single crochet * 3 times, * dec, 3 single crochet * 3 times

Crochet 9 single crochet, * 2 single crochet, dec * 3 times, * dec, two single crochet * 3 times, 11 single crochets, two ink, four single crochets

Repeat from * through row 42, working nine single crochet, one decrease, one single crochet, three decreases, one single crochet, three decreases, one single crochet, three decreases, twelve single crochet, two increases, five single crochets.

Nine single crochet, six dec, 14 single crochet, two hc, five single crochets = Row 43.

Row 44 comprises six single crochets, a decrease of six stitches, thirteen single crochets, an increase of six stitches, and six single crochets.

After that, make a knot and leave a long tail for sewing. After that, stuff the body and use a tapestry needle to seal the hole at the feet, exactly as it's shown in the photographs.

FEET

We crochet two sets of feet for the dinosaur using the same color of yarn as the head and body of the dinosaur. It is important to note that the pattern for both feet is similar up to row 6, after which it starts to diverge. After that point, the design begins to change. Take note of the highlighting in the following.

Rounds worked in single crochet in the middle row

The sixth iteration of the pattern in row 1 is the beginning of the first increment.

Work an increase followed by one single crochet stitch in the second row. Then work two single crochet stitches, four double crochet stitches, four double crochet stitches, and one single crochet stitch

The following is the design for the third row: 4 single crochet stitches, two increase stitches, one single crochet stitch, two increase stitches, six single crochet stitches, ink, one single crochet stitch

Work 22 single crochet stitches into the back loop of the stitch being worked only on the fourth row

Twenty-two single crochet stitches are counted in row 5.

5 single crochet, 5 dec, 5 single crochet, 5 dec = Row 6 (16)

TAKING A STEP WITH YOUR RIGHT TO:

Row 7: Work (4 single crochet, four dec, four single crochet) 12 times, turning after the last chain stitch.

Row 8 is worked in single crochet seven times

FOOT REMAINING:

Seventh row: chain 1, four single crochets, decrease by one stitch four times (for a total of eight); chain 1, turn

A decrease is worked into the eighth row, which consists of five single crochet stitches

Prepare the tail for use in a seam by stuffing it, closing it, and securing it.

ABDOMINAL PATCH

Make a green crochet dinosaur out of blue yarn, a pink crochet dinosaur out of pink yarn, and a blue crochet dinosaur out of green yarn.

Ch 11

In the first row, chain two and then stitch ten single crochets into the second chain from the hook. Turn the work and chain 1.

Chain 1, turn; increase by eight stitches, single crochet by 3, increase by 12 stitches, chain 1. This completes Row 2.

Chain 2, make 14 increases, single crochet 10, 14 more increases, chain 1, turn.

Fourteen single crochet stitches worked in rows four through eight, one chain stitch, and one turn.

Row 9: Decrease 12 single crochets (13), chain one, and turn.

Decrease by making 11 single crochets, 12 double crochets, and turning row 10.

In Row 11, you will reduce by single crocheting eight stitches, decreasing by ten times, and turning.

Reduce by one stitch, work six single crochets, reduce by one stitch (x 8), chain 1, turn; Row 12

Row 13: Decrease, four single crochets, decrease by six, chain one, turn.

Reduce by two single crochets, then reduce by four stitches, chain one, and turn; row 14

After you have finished fastening off, you should leave a long tail for sewing.

CRAFTY DINOSAUR FINGER GUNS

Construct the second one with the top and bottom sections made from the same skein of yarn. You are not allowed to stuff!

Rounds worked in single crochet in the middle row

Work three increases and three single crochets throughout Row 1, beginning at the bottom of the row.

Work 2 single crochet stitches, an increase of 3 stitches, and then four single crochet stitches in the second row

Work five single crochets into the third row, followed by an increase of two single crochets and five more single crochets

In the fourth row, work five single crochets, three double crochets, and three single crochets

Follow this pattern for the rest of Row 5: 2 single-crochet, three double-crochet, three single crochet

On rows 6 and 7, there are eight single crochet stitches.

In the eighth row, take out four spaces

After you have finished fastening off, you should leave a long tail for sewing. Follow the directions in the picture to fold the arm into a "scoop" configuration and stitch along the edge.

DINOSAUR PARTS FOR THE AMIGURUMI

The feet are the first part of the body to be attached. The toy's center of gravity may move somewhat depending on how much stuffing you put in the belly. As a result, you may need to experiment with different foot placements to keep the toy stable. Pins may be used to help you figure out where on your crochet dinosaur the feet will be the most secure (i.e., not fall). Attach the belly track to the belly in the next step. Again, securing it first could make it easier for you to decide where the best spot is to put it. At long last, the forearms of Dino should be inserted.

You may give your crochet dinosaur individuality by giving his nose a wrinkle. This is something you can do if you wish to do so. Pinch the toy in the appropriate places to create the form, and then use yarn close to the body color and a tapestry needle to stitch around it (but not too tightly).

SPIKES

XS, S, M, and L are the four different sizes of spikes that we make. Make a green dinosaur out of blue yarn, a pink dinosaur out of pink yarn, and a pink dinosaur out of green yarn.

Seven times the amount of XS sizes available:

Ch 2

In the first row, create one single crochet stitch (1) in the second chain from the hook, followed by one chain stitch, and then turn the work.

Row 2: enlargement (2)

Finish by leaving a tail for sewing, and then secure the end.

A spike in the form of an S with six sides:

Ch 2

In the first row, create one single crochet stitch (1) in the second chain from the hook, followed by one chain stitch, and then turn the work.

Row 2 represents an increment of 2 chain stitches and one turn.

On Row 3, make an increase of one single crochet stitch

Finish by leaving a tail for sewing, and then secure the end.

A spiral with a magnitude M that is repeated twice:

Ch 2

In the first row, create one single crochet stitch (1) in the second chain from the hook, followed by one chain stitch, and then turn the work.

Row 2 represents an increment of 2 chain stitches and one turn.

Row 3: Chain 1, three increases in single crochet, one single crochet, chain 1, turn.

To create an increase, crochet together two single stitches at the beginning of the fourth row (4)

Finish by leaving a tail for sewing, and then secure the end.

Two-piece spike in the form of an L:

Ch 2

In the first row, create one single crochet stitch (1) in the second chain from the hook, followed by one chain stitch, and then turn the work.

Row 2 represents an increment of 2 chain stitches and one turn.

Row 3: Chain 1, three increases in single crochet, one single crochet, chain 1, turn.

Row 4: Increase by crocheting two single stitches, then working four double crochets, and turn.

In Row 5, make an increase of three single crochets

Finish by leaving a tail for sewing, and then secure the end.

If you start at the top of the head, you should order the sizes of the spikes on the body as follows: S, M, 2x L, M, S, 3x XS, 4x S, and 4x XS.

a dinosaur egg that has been created using the craft of crochet

It is possible to split the egg in half, exposing the top and the bottom parts. In addition, if you want to crochet a green dinosaur, you should use yellow yarn, and if you're going to crochet a pink dinosaur, you should use violet yarn.

CONTOUR OF AN EGG

rounds worked in single crochet in the middle row

The sixth iteration of the pattern in row 1 is the beginning of the first increment.

You will do an increase with single crochet in the second row, and then you will repeat the previous pattern five more times

The following pattern will be repeated three times in Row 3: * single crochet two, increase * (24)

In the fourth row, you will increase by doing single crochet three times. This will be done six times (30)

Starting with row 5, you will single crochet four times, then increase six times (36)

For the sixth row, the pattern is as follows: * 5 single crochet, increase * six times (42)

In the seventh row, you will work an increasing pattern consisting of a sequence of single crochets of six stitches each

In the eighth row, you will increase your stitch count by single crocheting 11 stitches four times

You will single crochet 12 and increase four times on the ninth row

In the tenth row, you will increase your stitch count by single crocheting 13 times

In rows 11-15, there are 60 single crochet stitches.

You will single crochet 13 times, then reduce your stitches by four times in the 16th row

Repeat rows 17 and 18 with a total of 56 single crochets

You will reduce by four each time on row 19, starting with a single crochet 12.

On rows 20 and 21, there are 52 single crochet stitches

In the remaining portion of Row 22, * subtract 11 single crochets * four times

Work 48 single crochet stitches in Rows 23 and 24 of the patterns

Repeat Row 25 by working the following way six times: (2 slots, hc, dc, two tables, dc, hc)

Weaving in the ends of the yarn after they have been joined together.

EGG CAP

rounds worked in single crochet in the middle row

The sixth iteration of the pattern in row 1 is the beginning of the first increment.

You will do an increase with single crochet in the second row, and then you will repeat the previous pattern five more times

The following routine will be repeated three times in Row 3: * single crochet two, increase * (24)

In the fourth row, you will increase by doing single crochet three times. This will be done six times

Starting with row 5, you will single crochet four times, then increase six times

In the sixth row, work the following pattern: (single crochet 11, increase) three times

You will single crochet 12 times, then increase three times on the seventh row

To finish Row 8, work 42 single crochet stitches in a row

In the ninth row, you will raise your stitch count by three times by single crocheting 13 stitches

You will work 45 single crochets into the eleventh row of the pattern

The pattern for Row 11 is as follows: * 14 single crochets, increase * three times

Forty-eight rows worked in single crochet (12–20).

Weaving in the ends of the yarn after they have been joined together.

After inserting the crocheted dinosaur into the egg, you should cover the egg's bottom with the top.

Afterward, you may make a bow by attaching the different edges using a tapestry needle and scraps of yarn to form the bow's shape.

Whale

Dear Knitters and Crocheters, Greetings! I've been working on a new toy for quite some time now, and now I'd want to demonstrate how to construct a little blue whale.

My whale is a part of my Nautical Amigurumi Collection, which includes a seagull, a lighthouse, a sea star, a life belt, and a bevy of colorful lobster buoys. This collection inspired my love of the ocean and all things nautical.

Materials:

a yarn of medium weight consisting of turquoise and white (Lace 4)

The only additional components are a filling made of polyester fiber and two safety eyes measuring 9 millimeters in diameter.

3.5 millimeters is the size of the hooks.

A few often-used abbreviations and stitches are as follows: Mr. stands for the magic ring; chain stands for chain; sly set stands for slip stitch; single crochet stands for single crochet; dec stands for decrease; ink stands for increase; bl o is for back loop alone, and f/o stands for the completed object.

WORK IN ROWS, connecting each end with a slip stitch and ch1 unless otherwise advised. Work is joined to the previous row with a slip stitch.

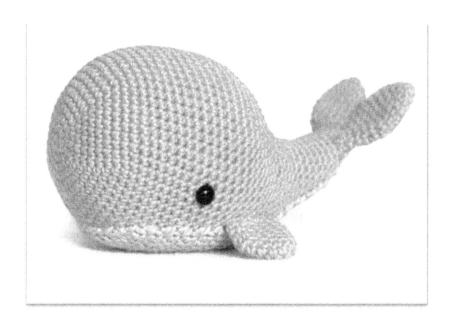

ZZ TWIST, a yarn produced by Lion Brand

Needle for crocheting: Clover Amour, 3.5 inches long

Polyester fibers are used for filling.

Eyes Made of Plastic Designed for Safety Precautions

BODY (turquoise and white yarn) (turquoise and white thread)

Using the turquoise yarn, make eight single crochets into a magic ring stitch

Two) an increase in the level of the area

Start with single crochet, then work an increase, and repeat around

Single crochet two additions, continue this pattern around the circle (32)

Start with chain 3, ink *, rapt ** around (40)

Sixth) Ch 4, ink, chain 4, repeat ** around (48)

Make single crochet with five increases, then repeat about ** times

8-17), work a row of single crochet in a straight line (56), and then insert the plastic eyes into the area between rounds 15/16. (About 15 stitches apart)

sc7, dec, rep ** around, sc2

Switching to a white yarn while continuing to work in single crochet

With BLO, *3 single crochet, dec*, repeat ** around

sc2, dec, repeat ** around

[single crochet, reduce, single crochet] around (20), repeat **; stuff the doll.

Procedure:

Work double crochet around (5), finish, close the hole and weave in the ends.

Include some needlework with white thread on the two lines below the eyes.

FINS (turquoise yarn; create two) (turquoise yarn; make two)

Work five stitches in a Mr. set

and increase the level of the area

Make single crochet, then an increase, and repeat about ** times

4–6 stitches in even single crochet, depending on the gauge

**around (10); fasten off and leave a tail of yarn to sew the fin to the side of the body; 7) *4 single crochets, decrements*, repeat **around (10);

TAIL (turquoise yarn) (turquoise yarn)

Double it:

Make six single crochets into a Mr. (6) (6)

Single crochet, increase, repeat around ** times

Thirdly, all you need to do to complete this step is to keep repeating the pattern "3 single crochet, increase" around the whole perimeter

Start with a chain four and a raise (*single crochet 4, chain 1), then repeat ** all around

Continue to repeat rounds (*sc5, sc2tog, ch2) all around. **

Crochet in rows that are even and single (14)

Chain five, decrease twice; chain five, repeat around **

sc4, dec, repeat ** around (10); F/O and cut yarn

Do not cut the yarn after you have completed the second fin; instead, chain one.

Bring together the two components:

Attach yarn to the second fin using a slip stitch; chain one and single crochet in the same stitch; repeat from * across; three single crochets, one decrease, and four single crochets; continue across the other fin; repeat from * across;

One single crochet, Dec, repeat ** around (12)

Numeral Eleven) Even Single Crochet

increase, *1 single crochet*, repeat about ** times

2 single crochet, increase, repeat ** around (24); carefully stuff this portion of the tail, excluding the two fins.

14) Work 24 even rows of single crochet; when finished, fasten off and leave a long tail to connect to the back of the body (between rounds 18 and 20).

POUR WATER Into the Spray Bottle (white yarn)

Work eight single crochet into a Mr. set

Work 8 single crochets in the blow

Start with chain 2, dec, single crochet 2, repeat around **

Moreover, an even number of single crochet stitches for the fourth step

Fifth) Work four single crochets into each stitch around

Six double crochet stitches worked into the next stitch, and each stitch around (48); complete the project, weave in ends, and hide yarn.

You may sew the water spray onto the rear of the whale by using some white yarn.

UNICORN

The difficulty level is considered to be moderate.

An Instructional Crochet Pattern for "Jazzy the Unicorn"

Materials:

Hook size E (3.5mm)

The screws for security have a diameter of 15 millimeters

Needle for yarn

The Stuffing Is Made of Fiber

Evaporating pen (optional – buy here)

Yarn (acrylic, weight 4) (acrylic, weight 4)

White (I used CSS – White) (I used CSS – White)

Multicolor (I used CSS – Times Square) (I used CSS – Times Square)

Gold (I used Mary Maxim Starletta Sparkle – Topaz) (I used Mary Maxim Starletta Sparkle – Topaz)

"chain" or "chain stitch," respectively.

The most elementary form of crochet, which also happens to be the world's most basic form

"Back loop only" is what "BLO" stands for in its acronym form.

invisible decline

Techniques for Shaping the Eyebrows

Procedure:

Create a strand of yarn that is about 18 inches long "long. You first need to thread your yarn needle with one end and then use the other to create a large, snug knot.

Before connecting the safety eyes, you must first thread your needle into the back of the skull and stitch in between the two locations that have been assigned (marked with strands of yarn).

When a strand of yarn is stretched, dimples appear on the string's surface. Create a knot with the yarn end and tuck it inside the hat.

Instructions for working with the existing hair to create the mane and tail of the creature

How to Crochet a Horse, Unicorn, and Zebra Manes and Tails

How to Crochet a Horse, Unicorn, and Zebra Manes and Tails (An Amigurumi Tutorial)

The Step-by-Step Guide to Crocheting a Unicorn, Zebra, and Horse Mane (and Other Animals)

How to Crochet a Horse, Unicorn, and Zebra Manes and Tails

First, bring the size down to ten. "You can see that I only rooted hair on every other round in the fourth picture above, but I filled in the gaps with one strand of yarn on each side. The number of strands of string you use is a matter of personal preference, although I used well over a hundred.

When you wrap yarn around a book or DVD cover many times and then cut it at the top, it is simple to get precise cuts of the thread. This technique helps make blankets and other items.

Alternatively, you could use a ruler and a marker with disappearing ink to draw a rectangle on the head to serve as a guide for where to root the mane, and you could do the same thing for the tail by removing something circular that is approximately 1.5 times the length of the bottom. These options are viable "on the reverse side (measured in diameter).

Second, with the right sides together, insert your hook under a stitch at the top or bottom of the head or body. This will be done with the wrong sides together. A loop may be created by first catching the yarn on your hook and drawing it through, followed by grabbing the tail ends of the adventure and pulling them through the loop.

Third, if the person receiving the braid is a child, you should make a knot at the end of each hair strand to prevent it from unraveling.

Instructions

Head

Employing just white yarn to create:

After completing a foundation chain of 5, work an increase into the second chain from the hook, single crochet two times, and then single crochet five times into the last chain of the foundation chain. Continue around the opposite side of the chain by working two single crochets, followed by three single crochets, into the last chain stitch [14].

increase the stitch count by one, single crochet four times, increase the stitch count by three, single crochet four times, increase the stitch count by two [20]

double-increase, six-single-crochet, double-increase, six-single-crochet, double-increase, six-single-crochet, double-increase, six-

the sequence of 8 single crochet increases worked in a row, followed by two single crochet increases worked in a row

Work 10 increases in single crochet, then work two increases in double crochet, then work ten increases in single crochet, then work two increases in double crochet.

chain 12, *single crochet 2* twice, chain 12, *single crochet 2* twice

(Single crochet ten, plus four)

chain 3, reduce, single crochet 6, decrease, chain 3, repeat from *five times* until no more decreases occur.

Single crochet, 5 dec

single crochet 2, dec, five single crochet dec, single crochet 2

12. using a single crochet stitch in each of the surrounding stitches

Beginning with single crochet, work an increase as follows: (a single crochet 4, an increase * 5 times, a single crochet 2, finish with a single crochet 2)

Work five stitches together, increasing

[48] Begin with a single crochet 3, complete an increase, repeat the pattern four more times: *single crochet six expansions*, and finish with a single crochet 3.

Increase the number of stitches in the single crochet by 7

Single crochet four stitches in a row, then increase by working five repetitions of *single crochet eight + increase* in the next row.

18 - 27. Create a circle around [60] using a single crochet stitch.

Begin with four single crochet stitches, decrease by 1, and repeat the pattern five times: *7 single crochet stitches, reduce by 1*, then finish with four single crochet stitches.

*Dec in single crochet, using the number 7*chain 3, reduce, single crochet 6, decrease, chain 3, repeat from *five times* until there are no more decreases.

*Single crochet, five dec*single crochet 2, dec, five single crochet dec, single crochet 2

Now is the moment to use just three-quarters of our mental power. The sewing between the two spots you've picked will let you create the indentations for the eyes. First, the backings should be placed on the safety eyes, and then the eyes should be inserted.

Single crochet, 3 dec

Start with single crochet, decrease by one, and repeat the following pattern five times: *2 single crochet, dec*, then finish with single crochet.

single crochet that removes the crown

Put the stuffing in its place.

. reduce by one stitch the total number of stitches around

Put an end to all of this chaos.

Ears (make 2) (make 2)

Employing just white yarn to create:

To begin making a magic ring, work six single crochet stitches into the middle circle.

Make an increase in the single crochet stitch

chain one, work an increase, then chain two, repeat the previous instruction, ending with chain one [12].

. You may make an increase by completing three rows of single crochet

. row 2 single crochet, increase by two single crochets, repeat row 4 single crochet increase again, row 2 single crochet

Single crochet, increase by 5 at position

a one crochet stitch into each gap between the spaces in the [21] pattern.

reductions worked in single crochet totaling 5

chain 2, decrease, chain 4, reduce twice, chain 2, finish with a chain two decrease.

[12] *single crochet, 3 dec*

Crochet a single stitch into each stitch all the way around

After you have cut the yarn, be sure to leave a long tail for sewing. After closing it with a slip stitch, the top should have a half-fold made in it first.

Horn

A thread made of gold:

Construct a magic ring and work three single crochet stitches into it [3].

Around, increasing by one stitch every four until you reach the desired size.

Make an increase in the single crochet stitch

Work a single crochet stitch into each stitch around the object's circumference.

. Single crochet followed by two increases

Crochet a single stitch into each stitch all the way around

After you have cut the yarn, be sure to leave a long tail for sewing. A pack containing a lot of filler is made of fibers.

Body

Employing just white yarn to create:

To begin making a magic ring, work six single crochet stitches into the middle circle.

increase the number of stitches in each row by

Make an increase in the single crochet stitch

Make single crochet your first stitch, then work an increase, followed by five iterations (single crochet 2, growth).

 (To make the item more significant, do single crochet over the next three stitches)

Beginning with single crochet, work an increase as follows: (a single crochet 4, an increase * 5 times, a single crochet 2, finish with a single crochet 2) [36].

Work five stitches together, increasing

Begin with a single crochet 3, complete an increase, repeat the pattern four more times: *single crochet six expansions*, and finish with a single crochet 3.

Increase the number of stitches in the single crochet by 7

Single crochet four stitches in a row, then increase by working five repetitions of *single crochet eight + increase* in the next row.

Create a circle around [60] using a single crochet stitch.

 Begin with four single crochet stitches, decrease by 1, and repeat the pattern five times: *7 single crochet stitches, reduce by 1*, then finish with four single crochet stitches. Insert a single crochet stitch into each stitch around the circumference.

Dec in single crochet, using the number 7

Work a single crochet stitch around the circumference [48].

Chain 3, reduce, single crochet 6, decrease, chain 3, repeat from *five times* until there are no more decreases. [42]

. Put a crochet hook with a single eye into the top loop of each stitch around [42].

Single crochet, 5 dec

completing a single crochet stitch into each stitch all the way around [36]

using a single crochet stitch in each surrounding stitch [30].

Single crochet, 3 dec

After you have cut the yarn, be sure to leave a long tail for sewing—a pack containing a lot of filler made of fibers.

Arms (make 2)

A thread made of gold:

To begin making a magic ring, work six single crochet stitches into the middle circle.

Increase the number of stitches in each row by [12].

Make an increase in the single crochet stitch [18]

Make single crochet as your first stitch, then work an increase, followed by five iterations

"BLO" refers to doing a "single crochet in each stitch around."

Work a single crochet stitch into each stitch around the object's circumference.

Alter your pattern so that it uses white yarn as your guide:

Putting a single crochet stitch into each existing stitch all the way around

Crochet 11 rows of single crochet, then decrease by one stitch and finally crochet 11 rows of single crochet.

Work a single crochet stitch around the circumference

single crochet 21, dec [22] single crochet

Create a single crochet stitch between the [22] stitches in each space.

Single crochet ten rows, then decrease by ten rows, ending with a chain 0.

a one crochet stitch into each gap between the openings in the [21] pattern.

Using a single crochet stitch in the surrounding stitches [20].

Work nine single crochets after chaining 19 and turning [19].

A single crochet stitch into the space between each stitch [19]. [Crochet] [Single crochet stitch]

Insert a single crochet stitch into the middle of each corner double crochet.

After you have cut the yarn, be sure to leave a long tail for sewing. A pack containing a lot of filler is made of fibers. After closing it with a slip stitch, the top should have a half-fold made in it first.

Legs (make 2) (make 2)

A thread made of gold:

To begin making a magic ring, work six single crochet stitches into the middle circle.

Increase the number of stitches in each row by [12].

Make an increase in the single crochet stitch [18]

Make single crochet your first stitch, then work an increase, followed by five iterations of (single crochet 2, increase).

(To make the item more significant, do single crochet over the next three stitches) [30]

Single Crochet into each stitch around [30] using the back loop of the yarn alone (BLO).

07 - 08. using a single crochet stitch in each surrounding stitch [30].

Alter your pattern so that it uses white yarn as your guide:

Using a single crochet stitch in each surrounding stitch [30].

chain 14, subtract two from the total, then chain 14 [29]

27 dec [28] single crochet

chain 13, then a reduction, then chain 13 [27]

When working in single crochet, the 25th of December becomes the 26th.

Work 12 single crochet stitches in a ring, dec, and then work 12 single crochet stitches in a

row made with a single crochet stitch [December 24]

[23] Crochet 11 rows of single crochet, then decrease by one stitch and finally crochet 11 rows of single crochet.

Single crochet 21, dec [22] single crochet

Single crochet ten rows, then decrease by ten rows, ending with a chain 0.

19 Dec 20 single crochet single crochet

Work nine single crochets after chaining 19 and turning [19].

single crochet 17, dec [18]

Single crochet, minus seven dec

sc2, dec

Owl

Crochet thread in black, acrylic yarn in purple, cyan, white, and other miscellaneous materials. Two 4mm pink brads

Regarding a yellow felt seal is a significant concern

Materials:

a hook with a diameter of three millimeters

Needles for darning

Polyester fibers are used to construct the stuffing for the product.

Ch - Chain

A single stitch is performed in crochet.

"dc" is the acronym that stands for "double crochet."

The term "increment stitch" may also be shortened to "two single crochets in a stitch," and its abbreviation is "inc."

Invisible decline (or inv dec)

AMIGURUMI Owl Crochet Pattern to Download and Print

Body

In the thread of violet:

At the beginning of the first round, perform a scrimshaw six in the middle of the magic ring.

Procedure:

A number close to 12 should be added for the second round.

Work an increase and a single crochet stitch for the third round (18).

Work [ink, sc2tog] around the number 24 during the fourth round of the pattern.

Work [ink, single crochet 3] around the number 30 during the fifth round of the pattern.

In the sixth round, you will increase by two stitches, then single crochet around stitch 36 four times.

You should do double crochet around a 36 throughout rounds 7-18.

If you're following the pattern, round 19 is [Inv dec, single crochet 4], which equals around 30.

At about the 24 mark, complete 20 rounds of the [Inv dec, single crochet 3] pattern.

You will need to complete a [Inv dec, single crochet 2] for the 21st round as you work around the number 18.

Put useless things into your body.

[Inv dec, single crochet 1] should be worked around the number 12 during the 22nd round.

The [Inv dec] from Round 23 will begin to have an impact at about the number 6.

Complete the task and tuck away the loose ends.

Eyes

The second one, which makes use of white yarn, resembles this one:

At the beginning of the first round, perform a scrimshaw six in the middle of the magic ring.

A number close to 12 should be added for the second round.

Work an increase and a single crochet stitch for the third round (18).

After you have cut the yarn, be sure to leave a long tail for sewing.

Collect some black crochet thread, snip it into little pieces, and then stitch a diagonal eyelid over each of the eyes. Make a knot out of the two ends and tie it behind you.

Wings

The second one should be worked with cyan yarn and look somewhat like this.

At the beginning of the first round, perform a scrimshaw six in the middle of the magic ring.

A number close to 12 should be added for the second round.

Work an increase and a single crochet stitch for the third round (18).

After you have cut the yarn, be sure to leave a long tail for sewing.

Ears

A pair of yarn needles in a lilac color:

Row 1: Work a triple crochet stitch in the middle of the magic ring.

The second boost occurs sometime between 6 and 7.

After you have cut the yarn, be sure to leave a long tail for sewing.

The Elements That Makeup Crochet, Along with Its Construction

Make sure you crochet all the parts by following the crochet pattern exactly.

Begin the Body by crocheting in a continuous circle.

For Rounds 7-18, work carefully around the [36] marker.

When you reach Round 21, you should start stuffing the body with polypill fiber.

First, you need to make two eyes, and then you may embellish them with a length of black crochet thread.

Stitches should be used to attach the eyes to the body.

Construct a set of wings and use some thread to secure them to the body when you've finished.

By folding the wings in half along their longitudinal axis, it is possible to give the impression that they are semicircles. Pass a needle and thread through each one, then stitch it onto the body so that it points in the direction of the bottom of each eye. 6a

Under the eyes, on the body, cut a length of cyan yarn and stitch a series of Vs. with the pointy side facing outward. The accurate answers are as follows: three on the top row, two in the center, and one at the bottom.

You may attach the ears to the head by stitching them onto the top of the head.

Make an adorable beak out of the yellow felt by using it. You need just cut it along the center to separate it into two halves. Position it so that it is squarely in the center of both of your eyes.

PIG

These adorable piglets are about the same size as actual pigs, which makes them the ideal size for being held and cuddled.

Materials:

(A) Knit Picks' Wool of the Andes Super wash Bulky in Blossom Heather, (B) Oyster Heather, and (C) Mineral Heather; correspondingly, the nose, the main body, and the spots.

Hook made by Furls and part of their Alpha Series. Olivewood construction. Size G (4.0mm) or G+ (4.5mm)

Stuffing

The eyes are plastic clips that measure 10 millimeters.

Needle for tapestry work or yarn

Sewing pins and needles (optional)

Stitch identifier (I use a small scrap of yarn)

The initials "Ch" stand for the word "chain."

The abbreviation for single crochet is "Sc," and the corresponding symbol.

"dc" is the abbreviation used for double crochet.

Dc dec = decrease in a double crochet stitch

Slip stitch is an abbreviation used to refer to a slip stitch.

Sc equates to skipping

F.O. – to finish

Rep stands for repetition.

Decline = decline

PM = location indication

The symbols for the number of times, such as two times, three times, etc., are written as 2x, 3x, etc.

Procedure:

The pig's head and torso are covered in the first section of the CAL. The pig's ears, legs, and tail will be covered in the second portion of the CAL (the bottom is considered part of the body!).

Since the spots on each pig are unique colors, the pattern does not come with any color charts to refer to while working on it. Add a dash of color anywhere you think it would look good! If you have difficulty following the pattern, you may find it helpful to begin by working on a piggy with a single color.

The Whole, the Nose, and the Face

Make three chains in color A using the stitch.

Two single crochets in the second chain space from the hook, four crochets in the final chain space while turning your work to work along the chain's underside (as shown), and two more crochets in the same chain space as the first two single crochets. This completes the first row of the pattern (8)

The pattern is composed of two single crochets in the first five stitches, a slip stitch (also known as a loose stitch) in the one that immediately follows it, and another single crochet in the last stitch (13)

Remove the marker, then do the following sequence: *3 double crochet in the first stitch, single crochet in the next three stitches*, repeat *-* around (leaving the last single crochet unworked)

The information we now have is as follows: It is broken down into rounds, and each one has its unique hue to represent it.

TRANSFORM into B-Raster format.

Put the marker away and, while holding the BLO, make a dec in the next single crochet, then two single crochets in the next single crochet, single crochet in the following two single crochet, a dec in the next three single crochet, single crochet in the next three single crochet, a dec in the next three single crochet, and single crochet in the final two single crochet

Single crochet in the first two single crochet, skip ten stitches, single crochet in the next stitch, skip two stitches, single crochet in the next stitch, single crochet dec in the last stitch

Slip stitch (loose) in the next seven double crochet, single crochet in the next seven double crochet, slip stitch (loose) in the last seven double crochet

Your pig snout seems dejected and ill-defined at this point.

Let's start to work on a solution to this problem together.

Reattach color A to the front loops beginning in the first stitch of circle four as follows:

FO after working a chain stitch once more, a slip stitch in the first two loops, another chain stitch, slip stitches in the following six loops, another chain stitch, SLP stitches in the final five loops, and terminating with a chain stitch. The present situation of things is as follows:

(Once again, we're going to emphasize the framework with a color that has a lot of vibrancy.)

If you are working with a crochet hook, you have two options: you may either knot the yarn ends together and weave them in, or you can pull the thread ends through to the back and tuck them under the snout. That settles it! The pattern that was previously set may now continue.

Beginning with single crochet in each of the first three single crochet, work the following pattern: *2 single crochet in the next single crochet, single crochet in the next single crochet, single crochet in the next single crochet*, single crochet in each of the next eight single crochet, repeat from *-*, single crochet in each of the last three single crochet

sc2 in the first single crochet, sc1 in the next three single crochet, *sc2 in the next two single crochet*, repeat from *-* all the way through. Sc in each of the last two single crochet stitches six times

a single crochet stitch should be worked into the first A single crochet is worked into the first stitch, double crochet into the next stitch, ten single crochets, three repeats of "2 single crochets into the next stitch, a single crochet into the next stitch," and ten single crochets into the last 11 stitches (35)

Single crochet stitch in the first stitch, followed by two single crochet stitches in the next stitch, five single crochet stitches in the next stitch, *two single crochet stitches in the next stitch, single crochet in the next stitch, single crochet in the next stitch*, 20 single crochet stitches in the following row, repeat from *-*, single crochet stitch in the last two stitches (40)

crochet in each of the first 16 single crochets, decrease in the next single crochet, single crochet in the next two single crochets, repeat from *-* three times, drop in the next single crochet, single crochet in the last nine single crochets (41)

to crochet a single stitch into the very first stitch of every single crochet around

A single stitch should be crocheted into the first 14 stitches, followed by *2 single crochets in the next single crochet, single crochet in the next two single crochets, single crochet in the next single crochet*, single crochet in the following 11 stitches, repeating from *-* once more, and ending with a single crochet into the final nine stitches

Insert a single crochet stitch into each stitch all the way around

Insert the snap-in eyes between rounds 11 and 12 of the project. The left eye should be positioned to cover the reductions on the left side of the face and sit between the contractions on that side of the face. The right eye should be set so it sits slightly above the reductions on the right side of the face (see picture).

(Can you see the alterations that have taken place in the region just below your right eye?)

Make a single stitch of crochet in each of the first two stitches, then make *2 single crochets in the next single crochet, single crochet in each of the following four single crochets*, repeat from *-* four more times, then chain 3, turn

single crochet in the first seven double crochets, *2 single crochet in the next single crochet, single crochet in the next four single crochet, single crochet in the next two single crochet*, single crochet in the following 33 double crochets, rep *-* once more, single crochet in the last double crochet

First 19 single crochets in ring, dec the round, single crochet in next set, dec ring, single crochet in next 11 set, dec ring, single crochet in last 11 set First 19 single crochets in the round, dec ring, single crochet in next 11 set, dec ring, single crochet in last 11 set

Start with single crochet in the first 20 stitches, decrement in the following 18, repeat in the last 12 stitches, and end with single crochet in the previous stitch

to crochet a single stitch into the very first stitch of every single crochet around

You will now crochet a single stitch in each of the first two stitches, followed by a double stitch in the third stitch, a single stitch in the fourth stitch, and yet another double stitch in the fifth stitch. You will then crochet 19 single stitches, a decrement in a single stitch, five single stitches, a decrement in a single stitch, and 17 single stitches to finish

single crochet in the second chain from the hook, then [dc dec] in each of the next 23 single crochet.

Single crochet stitch in each of the next eight single crochet stitches, two single crochet stitches in the next single crochet stitch, a single crochet stitch in each of the next two single crochet stitches, a single crochet stitch in each of the following three single crochet stitches, and a single crochet stitch in the final three single crochet stitches

start with 13 single crochet stitches in the ring, then work two single crochet in the next single crochet, single crochet in the next two single crochet, two single crochet in the next single crochet, single crochet in the next 20 single crochet stitches, then work two single crochet in the next single crochet, single crochet in the next three single crochet, two single crochet in the next single crochet, single crochet in the last four single crochet stitches, and then work two single crochet in the first

Work a single crochet stitch in each of the first 11 stitches, followed by two single crochet stitches in the next stitch, a single crochet stitch in the next stitch, two single crochet stitches in the next stitch, a single crochet stitch in the next stitch, two single crochet stitches in the next stitch, a single crochet stitch in the next stitch, two single crochet stitches in the next stitch, and so on. *Work two single crochet stitches in the next single crochet, then work one single crochet stitch in each of the following four single crochet stitches. Repeat from * until the pattern is complete. Work two single crochet stitches into the next single crochet stitch, going through both loops as you go. Single crochet in each of the 17 single crochet stitches that are left

Insert a single crochet stitch into each stitch all the way around (58)

One single crochet stitch should be worked into each of the first 29 stitches, followed by two single crochet stitches worked into the next stitch, then eight single crochet stitches, two single crochet stitches worked into the next stitch, and finally, 19 single crochet stitches worked into the final row

cram as much as possible into the pig's skull. After knitting the whole pig bean, you will need to perform some simple needle shaping to correct the bloated shape, but it will be well worth your time.

from 27 to 44, single crochet in the next single crochet around, single crochet in the last single crochet of

[Single crochet dec, single crochet in next nine single crochet] six times, single crochet in each of the previous three single crochet stitches

(Row 46) Work a single crochet stitch into each stitch all the way around

Decrease with single crochet, then single crochet in each of the next seven single crochet stitches; continue all the way around

Decrease by single crochet, single crochet in each of the following six stitches, and repeat from *-* around for

IMPACT the last pig with your whole might.

[dec in next single crochet, single crochet in next five single crochet] The following constitutes the pattern: four times, chain nine, slip stitch in the second chain from the hook, single crochet in the next chain, two single crochets in the last six chains (tail produced!), repeat within the brackets twice more

If, after finishing Round 49 as stated, the tail is not centered on the body in proportion to the face and snout, all you need to do to fix this is shift the bolded region of the pattern to the proper location.

Decrease with single crochet, single crochet in each of the following four single crochets, and repeat from *-* all the way around for fifty rows

Repeat the pattern of "single crochet dec, single crochet in the next three single crochet" around for a total of 51 rows

Decrease by crocheting a single stitch, then crochet a single stitch in each of the following two single crochets; repeat around (52 times)

Reduce with single crochet, single crochet in the next single crochet, and repeat from *-* all the way around

a ring of decks made with single crochet

FAO, which will have a significant lasting impact.

After using stitches to close any remaining gaps, continue pushing the needle through the body (this is why I like to use a long tapestry needle), and continue until you reach the face directly above one of the eyes.

After inserting the hook through the top of the single crochet stitch and pulling it through, the eye should be visible. Make a hole in the skin of the face with the needle, and then thread it so that it passes through the stitch that is precisely above the second eye. Make every effort to stay alive.

Place the needle back into the first side, then pull the yarn taut while being cautious not to yank it too hard. Keep an eye on the outcomes, and stop when you reach a point where you are satisfied with them. You'll be able to regain the charming demeanor you had before you stuffed the piggy.

Complete the pork bean by weaving in the end, and you'll have a fantastic-looking finished product!

HALLOWEEN GHOST

What a sweet and spooky little crochet ghost! The fact that he is so adorable makes up for the fact that he is not threatening. He has a height of only 6 inches and can be put together in a snap in a brief period. Small black safety eyes and a thin strip of black felt serve as his lips; if you don't have safety eyes, smaller circles of felt work just as well. Smaller circles of felt work just as well if you don't have any safety eyes. He was crocheted in the "amigurumi style," which requires crocheting in a continuous spiral without pausing to link rounds. This technique is named after the Japanese word for "crochet amigurumi." To assist him in standing up, he has a little bag at the base of the item stuffed with weighted stuffing beads. The arms are crocheted individually and then stitched on, but the legs, head, and torso are all worked into one piece beginning at the bottom and working their way up.

Materials:

Please provide the white yarn in the worsted weight (I used cotton yarn from Peaches and Cream)

Crochet hook size G

2 - 9mm safety eyes, black (or cut eyes from felt)

a little bit of black felt cut off in a piece

scissors

Needle for yarn

a square of fabric with a dimension of at least six inches.

Needles and thread for sewing are included in this package.

Glue for textiles or hot glue gun

A bag is now crammed with beads.

Procedure:

You first need to make a little weighted bag that you can position at your ghost's bottom. To do this, cut a circle out of your fabric scrap using the circular cutter to get a process that is 6 inches wide.

Make your way around the sphere with a running stitch. After finishing the circle of the object, you may create the shape of a bowl by tugging the thread to gather the fabric in the center. Put some stuffing beads inside to make it heavier, then close the zipper. Backstitching should be done many times through the area that has been gathered to fill in any gaps. Finish off by cutting the thread once you have tied a knot.

Insertion with a weighted core that is fluffy and spectral.

The body is then crocheted and completed.

It is highly recommended that you begin with the ring of power.

In the first round, you will chain 1, then double crochet six times within the magic ring (6 single crochet)

In the second round, you will work two single crochets into each stitch (12 single crochet)

For the third round, work [one single crochet in the first set, then two single crochets in the next] around. circularly recur (18 single crochet)

In Round 4, you will work a single crochet in the first two stitches and then double crochet in the next two. This will complete the round (24 single crochet)

[1 single crochet in each of the first three stitches, then two single crochets in the next] During the rest of Round 5, the circular recursion will continue (30 single crochet)

Single crochet into each stitch around for the sixth round of the pattern (30 single crochet)

Seventh Round: [work one single crochet into each of the first four stitches, then work two single crochets into the next] repeat cyclically (36 single crochet)

For rounds 8-11, work single crochet stitches into the gaps between the stitches all around. (36 single crochet)

In the twelfth circle, [work one double crochet in each of the first four stitches, then sc2tog]

circularly recur (30 single crochet)

For Round 13, single crochet into each stitch all the way around.

[sc2tog, one single crochet in the next two sets] for the 14th round. Circularly recur (24 single crochet)

Put something heavy into the ghost's empty stomach to scare it.

[1 single crochet in the first stitch, sc2tog] for the rest of the remaining stitches in the round. Repeat cyclically (16 single crochet)

Throughout Round 16, do a single crochet in the first and second stitches of the round. Repeat cyclically (24 single crochet)

Two single crochet stitches should be worked into the next stitch after the first three stitches of the 17th round. Repeat cyclically (30 single crochet)

Throughout rounds 18-20, single crochet in each of the stitches (30 single crochet)

In Round 21, [single crochet in the first three stitches, sc2tog] is the pattern to follow. Repeat cyclically (24 single crochet)

For the 22nd round, [single crochet in the first four stitches, sc2tog] is the pattern to follow. Repeat cyclically (20 single crochet)

[Work a single crochet stitch into the first three stitches, then sc2tog] for the rest of the 23rd round. Repeat cyclically (16 single crochet)

If you are using safety eyes, place them around three rows down after stuffing the ghost, and then continue pressing as you finish the other portions of the spirit.

For Round 24, work a single crochet stitch into each stitch all the way around. (16 single crochet)

[Single crochet in the first two stitches, sc2tog] is what you'll do for the last round of the project. Repeat cyclically (12 single crochet)

During the 26th round, you will work single crochet into each stitch all the way around.

In the 27th round, you will sc2tog six times (6 single crochet)

Following this, you will need to thread the end of the yarn through the top row and then crimp the very end of the rope to get the required form.

Forms Comprised of Spectral Appendages

Construct a set of limbs as follows:

In the first round, work a chain 1, then a single crochet six times in the magic ring (6 single crochet)

In the second round, you will work two single crochets into each stitch (12 single crochet)

Performing a single crochet stitch into each stitch around for rounds 3-5. (12 single crochet)

[1 single crochet in the first stitch, sc2tog] for the next six rounds. repeat cyclically (8 single crochet)

Single crochet into each stitch around for the Group 7 stitch pattern (8 single crochet)

After weaving in the ends of the thread, sew one arm to each side of the body at the indentation.

Put anything in the mouth of someone (and eyes if using felt to cut eyes). I opted for an oval form, but you could just as quickly put a smile on there if you wanted to. Cut two little circles out of the felt to construct the eyes.

Using felt and a substantial amount of adhesive to create the appearance of a ghost is the most effective method.

Treats for Halloween, including candy corn and ghosts

Your ghostly newborn needs a comfortable place to slumber. Therefore, the only thing left for you to do is find it. Have a frightful blast dressing him up for Halloween and incorporating him into your decorations.

CHRISTMAS ANGEL

Downloading one, you may get a free crochet angel pattern, an angel amigurumi, or an amigurumi nativity scene.

Materials:

You may use any other DK yarn if you don't have access to Hayfield Bonus DK (100% acrylic, 100g/280m), but you'll only need one ball of each of the following materials to complete the project:

Peaches

Sunflower

White

Gold-colored lurex thread made by DMC called Lumina (L3821)

Memory wire with DMC Color Infusions that has been plated in 24k gold (or alternative gold jewelry wire)

The stuffing for toys

In addition, there is a spool of black thread and needles for stitching.

Seeds and beads in black

Polyvinyl alcohol glue

Needles for tapestry

The thread may be used for a variety of needlework projects.

Crochet hook size 3.50mm

Crochet hook size 2.5mm

Procedure:

dc2tog Joining two double crochet stitches is accomplished by inserting the hook into the first stitch, looping the yarn around the theme, and bringing it through the second stitch. Wrap the string around the article, then draw it through all the chain loops.

The whole list of the notations we use is included in the abbreviations and conversions reference. Even though the design is written in British English, it may be easily adapted to American English according to the instructions.

The whole pattern is worked using a crochet hook measuring 3.5 millimeters unless otherwise noted.

Body

Make a crochet magic loop with the white yarn by following the instructions.

After beginning with a chain-1 loop, join with a slip stitch to the first double crochet stitch. 1 row of stitches

Start with a chain of one and then do two double crochet stitches in each stitch around. Join with a slip stitch to the first double crochet stitch. The total number of stitches will be twenty.

In the third round, start with a chain one, then work ten repeats of "2 dc in next set, dc in next set," and finish by attaching a slip stitch to the first dc you produced. This sentence will be embroidered a total of thirty times.

Ch 1, dc in each stitch, and ss to join at the end of the row (first dc). This sentence will be embroidered a total of thirty times.

To complete the fifth round, begin with a chain one space, then dc in the back loop of each stitch, then ss to the first dc to complete the connection.

Simply chaining 30 stitches and then putting a slip stitch into the first chain stitch is all required to create a loop large enough for your angel to perch atop your Christmas tree. After the sixth row, continue to stitch into each chain stitch without cramming the gap between them.

Sixth Round: Chain 1, double crochet in each stitch, then slip stitch to join (starting dc).

Following the instructions for Round 5, continue crocheting rows of double crochet until the height of your item from the base measures 5 centimeters. I am filling one's mouth with food over and over again.

In the next round, start with chain 1, then work (dc2tog, dc in the next three sets) six times, then join with a slip stitch to the initial dc. (There are 24 stitches)

In the next round, start with chain 1, dc in each stitch, and then ss to join (first dc).

Repeat these steps all the way around, and then connects with a slip stitch to the first dc you made. The total number of stitches will be twenty.

For the next round, start with a chain one, then work a double crochet in each stitch, and finish by making a single stitch into the top of the first double crochet you worked on.

You will chain one at the beginning of the next round and repeat the following instructions four times: (dc2tog, dc in next three stitches). There are a total of sixteen stitches.

In the next round, start with chain 1, dc in each stitch, and then ss to join (first dc).

dc2tog, dc in next two sets, repeat from * 4 times, connect with us to initial dc. This completes the pattern. A total of twelve stitches

In the next round, you will chain one and do a dc2tog six times before joining with a slip stitch to the initial dc. Count of stitches: 6

Stuff the body, ensure the entrance is tight, and leave a long tail so it can be closed.

Participation of the Upper Extremities (Hands and Arms)

For instance, in the second chapter of Peaches.

Work six double crochet stitches into the second chain from the hook in the first round, then connect to the first double crochet stitch with a single slip stitch.

Ch 1, dc in each stitch, and ss to connect at the end of each row (to join dc to ch1, do not turn).

Switch to the White View

The instructions for the fourth round are as follows: chain 1, then make a double crochet in each stitch around without connecting the stitches. Continue working in a spiral instead, but do not end the round with a single crochet stitch.

Before you finish the project, leave a tail of yarn long enough to stitch the arm to the body.

Construct a second arm and use stitches to join it to the body, so it hangs down from the top. First, sew the upper part of each arm to the body, and then sew the bottom portion to the body, stopping your stitching at 1.5 centimeters from the top of the arm.

If you're skilled with a pair of needles, you can make your crocheted angel a knitted friend to go along with her.

free knitting pattern for angels

Head

When trying to solve an issue, you use a top-down strategy.

Peaches will help you crochet a magic loop for your project.

First round: Chain 1, work ten double crochet stitches into the loop, and then join with a slip stitch to the first double crochet you created. 1 row of stitches

Start with a chain of one and then do two double crochet stitches in each stitch around. Join with a slip stitch to the first double crochet stitch. The total number of stitches will be twenty.

Start with chain one and dc in each stitch; join with a ss to the first dc.

Fourth Cycle This cycle is the same as the third one.

Repeat rounds 5-8, working dc in each stitch and connecting with a ss to the first dc each time.

In the ninth round, you will chain one, then perform (dc2tog, two dc) five times, linking each set of stitches with single crochet to the initial dc of the round. (Number of Stitches: 15)

After chaining one, you will double crochet twice together seven times, then single crochet into the next stitch before attaching with a slip stitch to the first dc you created in the previous round. This completes the tenth round. A total of eight stitches

Adjust the screw tension. Stuffing and stitches should be used to close the opening. Don't snip it off since you'll need that end for stitching later.

Hair

Using the Sunflower stitch, you may make a magic loop in crochet.

Start with a chain of one, then work six double crochet stitches into the ring. Join the first double crochet stitch using a slip stitch. Count of stitches: 6

Start with a chain of one and then do two double crochet stitches in each stitch around. Join with a slip stitch to the first double crochet stitch. A total of twelve stitches

For the third round, you will need to chain one, work two double crochets in the next stitch, and then double crochet in the following stitch six times in a row, and then join with a slip stitch to the first double crochet you worked. (Number of Stitches: 18)

Fourth Round: Ch 1, dc in each set around, link with ss to the first dc made in the previous round.

The fifth round is completed as follows: Ch 1, work two double crochets in the next stitch, then work two double crochets in the following stitch, repeat from * six times, then connect with a slip stitch to the first dc created. (There are 24 stitches)

Start with chain 1, dc in each stitch around, then ss to join.

Start with chain 1, then work a double crochet in the following 16 places. Turn.

It should be redone from the eighth to the thirteenth row.

Adjust the screw tension. Before sewing to the head, roll the hair's base up and secure it with bobby pins.

If you enjoy this free crochet angel pattern and are looking for more holiday crochet inspiration, you may also be interested in the following freeways: Top 20 Free Christmas Crochet Patterns; 61 Free Crochet Christmas Decoration Patterns.

A free amigurumi design for a Christmas pudding that you can crochet.

Wings (create two) (make two)

Simply chain six stitches and then slip stitch into the very first chain stitch to create a ring out of gold memory wire from DMC Color Infusions.

First row: Chain 3, work seven triple crochet stitches into the ring and turn.

Ch 7; tr in the first stitch (skip stitch at the base of chain set); chain 3; tr in next; chain 3; tr in next; chain 3; skip 2; dc in next; chain 3; skip 1; dc in next. Row 2: Ch 7; tr in the first stitch (skip stitch at the base of chain set); chain 3; tr in next; chain 3; tr in next; chain

Adjust the screw tension. Use a weave to connect any loose ends.

Halo

To make a ring, work 16 chains and do a slip stitch in the first chain of the first chain you worked. I worked with the gold memory wire from DMC Color Infusions. To create a " standing up halo," you must fasten it off, weave it in the ends, and attach it to the wearer's head in a single position at the back of their head.

Trumpet

Used a hook size of 2.5mm and 12 chains of DMC Lumina gold.

Creating the first row consists of working a double crochet stitch in the chain space that is two chains away from the hook, as well as in each chain space that is along the row, and then turning. That is a significant number of stitches. [11 total]

Row 2: Ch 1, then dc in each dc across. This completes the row.

When you are finished, be sure to leave a long tail.

Simply doubling the DMC Color Infusions wire length will allow you to create a gold wire that is precisely the same length as this crochet strip. The two ends of the wire should be twisted together, but a gap between them should be big enough for you to remove one of the strands and make a loop in the middle. It is going to act as the grip for the trumpet.

The bottom of the trumpet may be crafted by sewing the two long sides of the crochet strip together around the twisted wire while exposing the loop of the handle. This will create the base of the trumpet. Adjust the screw tension.

Horn blast

In crochet, you should make a magic loop,

Rend 1: Ch 1, work four double crochets in the loop, then slip stitch to the first double crochet to connect.

Continue to make spiral motions without pausing to ss after each cycle.

The first round will be repeated twice (2 double crochets in the next stitch and single crochet in the following stitch). Count of stitches: 6

Continue working a double crochet stitch into each stitch, as you did in Rounds 2 and 3.

Iterate Round 4 a further two times (2 dc in next, dc in next two sets). A total of eight stitches

It is necessary to repeat Round 5 four times, working two double crochets into the next stitch and one double crochet into the stitch that comes after it. A total of twelve stitches

Continue crocheting Round 6 another five times by working two double crochet stitches into the next stitch and a single crochet stitch into the one that follows it. (Number of Stitches: 18)

When working the seventh round, two double crochet stitches are inserted into each stitch. This has a total of 36 stitches in its construction.

Adjust the screw tension. Use the long thread to sew the trumpet's bell to the instrument's base.

Belt

It uses a hook with a size of 2.5mm and a gold DMC Lumina thread. Construct a chain about 30 centimeters; after it is complete, conduct one row of double crochet along the chain.

Tie a knot in any loose ends that you find. Wrap your arms around the angel and bind her up.

make amends

To build the nose, many stacked rows of straight stitches of varying lengths should be worked with Peaches. Attach two black seed beads to serve as the creature's eyes, and then use a length of black embroidery thread to backstitch on brows and a mouth. You may use standard sewing thread to connect the wings to the back, the hand to the handle of the trumpet, and the mouth to the base of the trumpet.

Printed in Great Britain
by Amazon

23573929R00136